"It is hard to capture the essence of the profound wisdom of this book. Francis Pring-Mill is a thoughtful and gentle guide to the ancient wisdom of the *Tao Te Ching*. His commentary combines beautiful prose and photography with a clarity that has come from a lifetime of living with this teaching. He invites us to meditate on the path of self-emptying and alignment with the Tao, the center around which all things turn as a path to the abundance and joy we all long for. I highly recommend this book for those who seek a peaceable way within themselves and harmony with others."

— Harry O. Maier, Professor of New Testament and Early Christian Studies, Vancouver School of Theology and author of *New Testament Christianity in the Roman World*

"*In Harmony with the Tao* is for lovers of the *Tao Te Ching*. It is obvious that Francis Pring-Mill has long studied the Tao. This book is thoughtful, rich in metaphor and illuminating. Savor this book and be guided into wholeness and oneness."

— Rick and Mary NurrieStearns, authors of *Yoga for Anxiety*, *Yoga for Emotional Trauma* and *Yoga Mind, Peaceful Mind*

"Francis Pring-Mill elucidates the ancient Asian wisdom of the *Tao Te Ching* so simply and clearly, you feel you are having a conversation with a friend. As we journey through tumultuous times, it is good to have a guide who sees the way of the Tao, acknowledges with compassion the difficulties we encounter, and points unswervingly to the deepest truth of existence. Step by delightful step, Dr. Pring-Mill leads us to willingly embrace the mystery of living *In Harmony with the Tao*."

- Linda Holiday, author of *Journey to the Heart of Aikido: The Teachings of Motomichi Anno Sensei*

In
Harmony
with the Tao

In Harmony *with the* Tao

A
Guided
Journey
into the
Tao Te Ching

Francis Pring-Mill

Including the Complete Text of Stephen Mitchell's
Tao Te Ching: A New English Version

All text from Tao Te Ching by Lao Tzu, A New English Version, with Foreword and Notes,
by Stephen Mitchell. Translation copyright © 1988 by Stephen Mitchell. Reprinted by
permission of HarperCollins Publishers.

Published by

Star
Lake
PRESS

www.inharmonywiththetao.com

Cover and interior design by Christy Day, Constellation Book Services

First edition: 2018
Reprinted: 2023

ISBN (paperback): 978-1-7387668-0-2
ISBN (ebook): 978-1-7387668-1-9
ISBN (hardcover): 978-1-7387668-2-6

Printed in the United States of America

The Library of Congress has cataloged the first edition as follows:

Library of Congress Cataloging-in-Publication Data
Names: Pring-Mill, Francis, writer of added commentary. | Mitchell, Stephen,
1943- | Lao Tzu. Tao Te Ching. English.
Title: In Harmony with the Tao : A Guided Journey into the Tao Te Ching / by
Francis Pring-Mill.
Description: Ashland, Oregon : White Cloud Press, 2018. | "Including the
Complete Text of Stephen Mitchell's Tao Te Ching: A New English Version."
Identifiers: LCCN 2018006586 | ISBN 9781940468693 (pbk.)
Subjects: LCSH: Lao Tzu. Tao Te Ching.
Classification: LCC BL1900.L35 P75 2018 | DDC 299.5/1482--dc23
LC record available at https://lccn.loc.gov/2018006586

Preface

How did I come to write this book? Like many people, I have been fascinated by the *Tao Te Ching*. I first came across it as a teenager. The book was not given to me, and no one had suggested I read it. Somehow I found a copy for myself, most likely in a secondhand bookstore. What I do remember is how I felt. It was as though someone had pulled me aside and whispered in my ear, "Psst. In case you've been wondering what life is all about, this is what's going on." Of course, there was no one there, but the words were clearly there on the printed page. And they were mine to read, again and again if I wanted. I felt I had discovered treasure.

I found out later that many people have discovered this treasure. The *Tao Te Ching* likely resonates for them as deeply as it does for me. And that is wonderful. However, I knew I wanted to spend more time with the text because, although the words resonated with me, I did not know why. The *Tao Te Ching* is short and concise, its sentences dense and cryptic. In places, the meaning is ambiguous and the words contradictory, and the mind struggles to understand the message.

While much of the message is in the words on the lines, it seemed to me that much more of the message lay between the lines. But what exactly was it that lay there? I wanted to know. At least, I wanted to know what was true for me. However, I also knew this would be a project that would take some time. And it was not obvious when I was going to get that time. However, a few years ago I retired from a career that included science, statistics, and information technology consulting. Finally, I saw some stretches of time opening up that I could call my own. I recognized my chance to spend time with the *Tao Te Ching*, and I took it.

The text of my "guided journey" is based on an existing English version of the *Tao Te Ching*. The original text by Lao Tzu is written in Chinese, and I am not a translator. For the purpose of this project, I have spent time with many translations and interpretations, some literal, others scholarly, philosophical, and poetic. I finally selected the well-known version by Stephen Mitchell. I agree with the words of religion scholar Huston Smith: "Mitchell's rendition of the *Tao Te Ching* comes as close to being definitive for our time as any I can imagine. It embodies the virtues its translator credits to the Chinese original: a gemlike lucidity that is radiant with humor, grace, large-heartedness, and deep wisdom."

Stephen Mitchell's version is my foundation. Without it, this book would not have been possible. I am deeply grateful to Mr. Mitchell for his support of the project and to HarperCollins for permission to reproduce all of his text. This book is laid out as follows: For each chapter, there is the text of the *Tao Te Ching* in Stephen Mitchell's words, followed by the text of my guided journey. This pattern repeats for each of the eighty-one chapters of the *Tao Te Ching*.

It must be said that the *Tao Te Ching* is a classic text of Chinese philosophy. So to write down what I think lies between the lines is a presumptuous undertaking and I accept all the responsibility that goes with it. Thus any inaccuracies in meaning are mine, as are any misunderstandings or misrepresentations. So for these shortcomings I apologize in advance. On the other hand, I hope to offer words that help present the central message in a less concentrated form. I believe the process of writing these words has helped me to better understand the *Tao Te Ching*. It is my hope that reading them may do something similar for you. If so, that's great and my purpose has been fulfilled.

In a nutshell, what is the *Tao Te Ching* all about? I think the answer is as follows: the *Tao Te Ching* is about the Tao, which is the great Oneness/Wholeness that encompasses everything. It is infinite and timeless. And we are part of it, although we spend much of our time imagining we are separate and alone.

The Tao is also continually unfolding, regardless of what we do. And we have a choice. We can either live in harmony with it or stand separate and apart and attempt to impose our will. If we do the first we live in peace and serenity; if we do the second we often live in confusion and sorrow. You might wonder, why would we do anything but the first? The answer, in a word, is desire.

When we live in harmony with the Tao, we empty ourselves of our own desires and the need to satisfy them. As a result, we do not try to impose our will. In fact, we do not "try" to do anything. The point isn't to achieve what we typically spend so much time striving for, that is, material possessions, security, and the esteem of others. The point is to live in harmony with the world around us. Peace and serenity follow; they are not goals to be strived for.

You might think this reduces our role to that of passive spectators. Not so. We do not watch the Tao unfolding, as it were. We are part of the unfolding. Our role is to act with compassion to guide and shape events as we let them come and go—without trying to hold onto them or bend them to our will. The difference is that we are centered in the Tao, not in ourselves.

What's more, each of us has a unique contribution to make. If you like, living in harmony with the Tao is like being at a concert, except that we're not in the audience. We're here to sing our song. And there is nothing passive about singing. But first we need to learn to listen, so we can hear the music all around us. Otherwise, when we listen only to ourselves and our desires, all we create is noise.

Each of us can add to the harmony. The saying goes, "Don't die with your song unsung." We are born to "sing" or at least with the opportunity to do so. In fact, I believe this is why we're here. Your song is unique and it is yours. So don't sit in the audience. Live in harmony with the Tao. I hope you enjoy what lies ahead in this book.

Francis Pring-Mill
Vancouver, BC

The tao that can be told
is not the eternal Tao.
The name that can be named
is not the eternal Name.

The unnamable is the eternally real.
Naming is the origin
of all particular things.

Free from desire, you realize the mystery.
Caught in desire, you see only the manifestations.

Yet mystery and manifestations
arise from the same source.
The source is called darkness.

Darkness within darkness.
The gateway to all understanding.

Our desire to know keeps us in the dark.

We're off to a puzzling start. We seek to understand. To understand something, we desire to speak about it. To speak about it, we have to name it. To name something is to identify it by distinguishing it from everything else. The trouble is, this doesn't work when we desire to speak about the eternal Oneness/Wholeness that is everything. When we try to name it, we discover we cannot because, in this case, we're trying to distinguish the thing that is everything from everything else. And if we cannot name it then we cannot speak about it. So how can we understand it? This is a good question. In fact, it stops the human mind dead in its familiar tracks. It's definitely puzzling.

If we think of Oneness/Wholeness as the only eternal reality, then the act of naming things is what distinguishes them, by making them into "particular things." These are obviously less than the eternal reality. "The name that can be named is not the eternal Name" precisely because we are able to name it. If that's the bad news, the good news is that at least we can talk about it. What's more, there's nothing wrong with naming things as long as we're aware of what we're doing and don't kid ourselves that we're talking about anything eternally real.

Why do we do this? We name, identify, and limit reality in separate artificial "manifestations" because we believe the only way to understand the whole is to understand the named parts. This is why we fail when we seek to understand the eternal Oneness/Wholeness, because it can never be understood in terms of parts, named or otherwise. Anything that's beyond understanding we call a mystery. Therefore the eternal reality is a mystery because it is beyond understanding.

But the fact that the eternal reality is beyond understanding does not mean it is beyond reach. Mysteries cannot be understood but they can be "realized." All we have to do is give up our desire to "know." As long as you remain "caught in desire, you see only the manifestations." While we can get to know the manifestations, we'll never understand Oneness/ Wholeness this way. In fact, the more we try, the more we will fail. It is only when you are "free from desire [that] you realize the mystery."

Where does all this come from? At the level of eternal Oneness/ Wholeness, both the real mystery and the artificial manifestations we create with our minds must "arise from the same source"—there's nowhere else for them to arise from. If we had to name it, we could call this source Beyond Knowing because it is on the other side of knowledge, as it were. This is where true understanding lies. The trouble is that with the eyes of knowledge we cannot see anything over there. It's all dark. "Darkness within darkness." It is the pursuit of knowledge that keeps us on this side of knowing. Thus the only way to get to the other side is to let go of the pursuit.

Letting go is like going past a point of no return only to discover that it is the "gateway to all understanding." To realize the mystery, all we have to do is go through the gateway. But this means letting go of our desire to name things and speak about them. With respect to the eternal Oneness/Wholeness, this means becoming aware and accepting that it's a mystery that simply is. It really doesn't matter that we cannot name it, because there's nothing to be said about it. On the other side of the gateway we fall silent. To dwell in this awareness is to realize the mystery.

Think of it this way. The Tao is real. Knowledge is illusion. It's certainly useful in its own domain, but no amount of it can ever lead us to realizing the mystery, because knowledge is all on this side of the gateway. In short, we can never understand the eternal Oneness/Wholeness in the sense of knowing it. We can never name it or speak about it, much less grasp it or possess it. But the point is that this doesn't matter. We can still realize it. To dwell in the Tao is to realize the mystery.

How often we find ourselves caught in the desire to know. We seem convinced that deeper analysis will enable us to understand something.

Have you ever simply been aware of the reality of a situation? You just know without knowing how you know. You likely can't even put your awareness into words. Or, if you could, you know the words wouldn't "do it justice," as we like to say.

This chapter reminds us that this is what realizing the "mystery" looks like. It is beyond things we can name with words. This is the "unnamable" that is eternally real. This is what it's like on the other side of the gateway. And, to our surprise, it is not dark. Can we describe it? No. So there is nothing to say. We're speechless. But the point is that we're in harmony with the Tao. Can we really live here? Yes.

2

When people see some things as beautiful,
other things become ugly.
When people see some things as good,
other things become bad.

Being and non-being create each other.
Difficult and easy support each other.
Long and short define each other.
High and low depend upon each other.
Before and after follow each other.

Therefore the Master
acts without doing anything
and teaches without saying anything.
Things arise and she lets them come;
things disappear and she lets them go.
She has but doesn't possess,
acts but doesn't expect.
When her work is done, she forgets it.
That is why it lasts forever.

The Tao makes no distinctions.

Here's why naming things causes us to lose sight of Oneness/Whole-ness. When we name something we immediately cause its opposite to spring into being. So now we have two things.

For example, when we name "beautiful," we cause people to distin-guish "ugly." Whenever we split out something by naming it and saying that it "is," we create its opposite, the "not-is" version. Here are some more examples: difficult and easy, long and short, high and low, before and after. None of them can be without implying their not-being version. Hence, "being and non-being create each other."

This is not necessarily a bad thing as long as we realize the limita-tion of what we are doing. The limitation, of course, is that at the level of the eternal Oneness/Wholeness there can be no opposites. There is only Oneness/Wholeness. To name something is to distinguish it from something else, and at the level of Oneness/Wholeness there is no "something else." Strictly speaking, even to name "Oneness" is to create the concept of "not-Oneness," which immediately means it is no longer Oneness, because the concept of not-Oneness is now out there as well.

However, while we cannot name Oneness/Wholeness, we can cer-tainly point to it. "Tao" is a good word for pointing to it. This is why "the tao that can be told is not the eternal Tao. The name that can be named is not the eternal Name" (chapter 1). The fact that the Tao cannot be named means it cannot really be spoken about, or therefore discussed, or therefore understood. Instead it's a mystery that can only be "real-ized." But more on this later.

In the meantime, now that we're aware that language creates artificial distinctions that are not real, what are we to do? Let's see what the Master does. The answer is that the Master does not "do" anything. This is because to do something is to identify the "something," which is to split it out from the Whole. Instead the Master simply "acts." Note that not doing anything is not the same as doing nothing. The Master doesn't "do nothing." She doesn't drop out. She is fully engaged in this world. The point is that acting is not the same as "doing things." Doing things involves expecting separate things to have particular, identifiable outcomes.

As soon as you stop doing separate things, you will find you can no longer name what you do. If you cannot name what you do, then you cannot speak about it. This is why the Master "acts without doing anything and teaches without saying anything." Her actions are her teaching. That's all there is to it. There is nothing to be said.

What does this look like in practice? It looks like this. When things arise you let them come. When they disappear you let them go. You do not try to hold onto them with your mind and possess them. Doing so is futile. You can indeed "have" but you can never "possess," because ultimately nothing is "yours." In the same way, "acting" does not involve expecting a particular, identifiable, nameable outcome. You simply act and let go. That's all there is to it. This is what the Master does. "She has but doesn't possess, acts but doesn't expect."

"When her work is done, she forgets it," because to remember it would involve identifying and naming it, which is to limit it and pin it down in time. Not pinned down in time, it lasts forever. This is what dwelling in the Tao looks like. This is the mystery being realized.

How often we make distinctions. Distinguishing one thing from another seems very important to us. Finding the right name matters a lot. Why? Because a lot hangs in the balance. Names are not neutral. If we call something good, we will strive for it. If we call it bad, we will avoid it. What's more, we will judge others according to what they strive for and avoid. And we have no shortage of names for one another.

Have you ever simply let things arise just as they are, with no names or judgments, and then let them go? When you do, you discover that things are simply what they are. When you no longer distinguish what you desire and what you seek to avoid, then something profound happens. Fear disappears. So do worry and regret.

This chapter reminds us that this letting go and this disappearance of fear, worry, and regret is what it's like when we dwell in the Tao. We let things come. We let things go. We respond without attachment to particular outcomes, without expectations. We are no longer separate and apart. We are part of the timeless flow.

3

If you overesteem great men,
people become powerless.
If you overvalue possessions,
people begin to steal.

The Master leads
by emptying people's minds
and filling their cores,
by weakening their ambition
and toughening their resolve.
He helps people lose everything
they know, everything they desire,
and creates confusion
in those who think that they know.

Practice not-doing,
and everything will fall into place.

Desire causes confusion.

Let's elaborate on what happens when we "do things" rather than simply "act." As we saw in chapter 2, doing things involves performing deeds with expectation of particular outcomes. What happens, if we're not careful, is that our motivation in doing them becomes to have the outcomes associated with the person who did them, that is, us (assuming we had in mind positive outcomes that we desire to be associated with). This prompts a couple of questions.

Who do we think is going to make the association? And why do we care? The answer is that we think other people will make the association. And we care because we desire that others think well of us. So here's a third question: Why do we want others to think well of us?

The answer matters because this thinking creates a serious problem. The problem occurs when we become motivated by what we think others will think of us. When we want others to think well of us, we have an ulterior motive, a hidden agenda. When this happens, our deeds become a means to an end, not an end in themselves. In other words, they're no longer done for their own sake but for the sake of what we think others will think. You may ask, what's wrong with this?

What's wrong is that when we look to others for direction, we no longer look within, to our own true selves. Instead, we take direction from the image we think others have of us—our self-image, or ego. In short, we become driven by our ego instead of listening to our self. And when we do this we give up our power, because we're now effectively controlled by what others think of us. As the first line of this chapter says, "If you overesteem great men, people become powerless." This is exactly what happens, and it causes all manner of conflict and difficulty.

Another example follows: "If you overvalue possessions, people begin to steal." In the Tao there is no such thing as mine and not-mine. (Of course, in the Tao there are no "things.") But if you think in terms of mine and not-mine and this leads you to overvalue possessions, then the obvious solution to desiring a possession that is "not-mine" is to forcefully take it for yourself. This is called stealing.

The point is, these problems originate in your mind with how you think. Will your desire to have others think well of you cause you to give up your power to the image you think they have of you? Will your desire for possessions cause you to steal because you want more things to be "yours"? Hopefully not. But how do you guard against these problems?

Here's what the Master does: "The Master leads by emptying people's minds and filling their cores, by weakening their ambition and toughening their resolve." The core is your self. Ambition is your ego. The Master has no ambition. But to live by taking direction from your self rather than your ego is difficult. It calls for constant awareness. So our resolve can indeed use all the "toughening" it can get. Excessive thought, knowledge, and desire are the source of all problems. So the Master helps people "lose everything they know, everything they desire." That should certainly help, although predictably this "creates confusion in those who think that they know." No kidding.

The key is not to "do" anything. Nor is it to do nothing. It is to "act." Pure action. No deed done with the expectation of an outcome designed to impress others. Just act and let go, as we saw in chapter 2. As it says here, "Practice not-doing, and everything will fall into place."

How often we seek to impress. When we do, our actions are not done for their own sake. They are done to produce specific effects on others. We desire to be esteemed. We long to be seen as one of the "great men." This is what matters to us.

Have you ever emptied your mind of expectation and desire? When you do, ambition, esteem, concern about the judgment of others—they all disappear. Your actions spring simply and naturally from your core. You are not trying to impress anyone. What's more, none of your power is sapped by wondering what others think.

This chapter reminds us that this power is at our command all the time. All we have to do is get out of our own way. When our ego steps aside, when our mind stops chattering and judging and worrying about the judgments of others, suddenly everything becomes simple. We do not need to "do" anything. We simply act. It is as though no effort is needed. Things just "fall into place."

4

The Tao is like a well:
used but never used up.
It is like the eternal void:
filled with infinite possibilities.

It is hidden but always present.
I don't know who gave birth to it.
It is older than God.

The Tao is without limit.

When we identify particular things either by naming them or by doing them, we cause particular possibilities to come into being. This means other possibilities are excluded. Whenever we do one thing we exclude the possibility of doing another thing. In an everyday, worldly sense this is inevitable because we cannot do every "thing" at the same time. But the point is that the Tao is not like this. It cannot be divided up into named constituent parts or possibilities. Nor does it exist at a particular moment in time. All of it simply is, all of the time. Everything is included. Nothing is excluded. Always.

Once again we see that the Oneness/Wholeness that is the Tao cannot be described. Any attempt to describe it involves paradox. For example, we could say the Tao is full of infinite possibilities. Or we could equally well say the Tao is a void, empty of all possibilities. Both are true. It doesn't matter. You pick.

If you pick the first phrase, then we might ask, how can anything be "full of" something infinite? The words fail. To be full of something implies a limit. A limit is finite. Something finite cannot contain something infinite. If there were a limit, then we could imagine that whatever the container is full of could be used up and the container could eventually become empty. The Tao is not like this.

If you pick the second, then the phrase "eternal void" captures it quite well. It does so better than the image of an empty container, because an "eternal void" can never be full. It can also never be used up. The Tao is more like this. Thus everything "uses" the Tao in that it exists within the Tao, but the Tao itself can never be used up. A bottomless well is a good image. "The Tao is like a well: used but never used up."

Things exist within the Tao and you can see them. But you cannot see the Tao itself. This is because you can see only certain things at a certain time and the Tao is everything everywhere, all of the time. Thus "it is hidden but always present." You are part of it. Has it always existed? Certainly it has. And it always will. It never came into being at a particular time. It always was.

To make this point, Lao Tzu jokes with us (I believe) in the next two lines: "I don't know who gave birth to it." This is surely said with a smile, because if the Tao has always existed, then it could never have been born. This joke shows again how words fail when talking about the Tao. They are too limited. Here's how they fail: "birth" implies "pre-birth"—in other words, a moment in time before something existed and then a moment later when it was suddenly "born." Of course the Tao is not like this. It is neither time-bound nor word-bound.

What's the oldest thing you can think of? Whatever it is, the Tao is older than that. Maybe your answer is God, whatever your idea of God is. In that case, the Tao "is older than God." Now do you understand? End of joke. The answer is that the Tao has no "age." Eternal reality has no beginning and no end. It just is.

How often we see limitations. How often we see only a few possibilities. When we are like this, we are separate and apart. What's more, we are trapped by the narrowness of our vision. The Tao is indeed hidden, but that doesn't mean it's not there. We simply cannot see it. Limitation comes only when we believe that what we can see is all there is.

Have you ever thought about the limitations of thought? Whatever's on the other side of thought is bound to be hidden. All that means is that we cannot know it and understand it. But that doesn't mean it is not real.

This chapter reminds us that although the Tao is hidden, it is always present. And, regardless of what we can or cannot see, we are never separate and apart. While we may see only limitations, in the reality of the Tao the possibilities are always infinite. They always have been. The Tao is like a well that never runs dry.

5

The Tao doesn't take sides;
it gives birth to both good and evil.
The Master doesn't take sides;
she welcomes both saints and sinners.

The Tao is like a bellows:
it is empty yet infinitely capable.
The more you use it, the more it produces;
the more you talk of it, the less you understand.

Hold on to the center.

The Tao is infinitely capable.

We have seen how the act of naming things creates their opposites. "Being and non-being create each other" (chapter 2). When we say that something "is," we create the "not-is" version. In the Tao there is only one version, the one that cannot be named. But if we insist on naming the versions, then the Tao is both of them.

However, having created two versions out of a single oneness, we frequently complicate the picture further by making judgments about them. We start to think one is "better" than the other. We think one version is "right" and the other "wrong." We are for one and against the other. We take sides.

In the Tao, of course, neither version exists, because there are no versions of anything, because there aren't any "things." But if we insist on creating versions, then not only is the Tao both of them, but also neither of them is better than the other. Neither one is right or wrong. It makes no sense to be for one and against the other. This is why "the Master doesn't take sides; she welcomes both saints and sinners."

In chapter 4 the Tao was likened to a bottomless well. This chapter gives us another interesting image. The Tao is not only everything that exists, it is also that in which everything exists. For example, in the world everything exists in air. In this respect, the Tao is like air: "It is empty yet infinitely capable." Air is not right or wrong. It just is. You cannot be for air or against air. Nor can you touch it, feel it, hold it, much less possess it. Yet you can use it, as in a bellows.

How do you use the Tao? You use it by acting in harmony with it. If you do this, it is as if "the more you use it, the more it produces." We say "as if" because, of course, this is not strictly true. The Tao doesn't "produce" anything. However, when you act in harmony with the Tao, it is as if something more has been produced. It's like using the air in a bellows to produce red-hot coals.

The final lines remind us again that living in the Tao is not about pursuing knowledge, naming things, and then talking about them. "The more you talk of it, the less you understand."

So what are we to do to understand? The answer is to forget pursuing the petty distinctions that miss the point. Go for the point. As the final line says, "Hold on to the center." The next few chapters will say more about what this means. In a nutshell, while we move in this world we need to remain centered in the Tao.

So, in saying this, did I just become trapped by my own words? Did I make a judgment? Quite possibly. I said, "We need to remain centered in the Tao." And you could say we don't really "need" to do anything at all. And you would be right. I should have said that if we move in the world while remaining centered in the Tao, harmony results and all manner of conflict and difficulty disappear. These are the rewards, as it were, of holding on to the center.

How often we like to talk, make distinctions, take sides, judge some people as saints and others as sinners. When we do this we forget we are limited by what we can wrap our minds around. Unlike the Tao, our minds are hardly "infinitely capable." In the grand scheme of things this means we can't wrap our minds around very much at all. Hence the more we talk, the less we understand.

Have you ever received acts of kindness from another? No talk, no explanation, just practical kindness exactly when you needed it? How true the phrase "Actions speak louder than words." This is capability in action producing results.

This chapter reminds us that the more centered we are in the Tao, the more capable we will be.

6

The Tao is called the Great Mother:
empty yet inexhaustible,
it gives birth to infinite worlds.

It is always present within you.
You can use it any way you want.

The Tao is yours to use.

We already know that "the tao that can be told is not the eternal Tao. The name that can be named is not the eternal Name" (chapter 1). But if you want to give it a name, "Great Mother" would do quite well. Why? Because it is as if it has given birth to everything that is. In giving birth it is like a mother. Since it has given birth to everything, we could even say it is like a Great Mother.

Again, note how we say it is "as if" because, of course, there was no time before the Tao, nor will there be time after it. The Tao exists outside time. It simply is. So, strictly speaking, there can be no moment of birth. So the image of a mother is a bit strained. However, given that we have to work within the limitations of language, "Great Mother" is not a bad fit.

We may recall, "The Tao . . . is like the eternal void: filled with infinite possibilities" (chapter 4). The idea here is the same. We are told the Tao is "empty yet inexhaustible" and that "it gives birth to infinite worlds." So we now have three images of the Tao: "The Tao is like a well . . ." (chapter 4); "The Tao is like a bellows . . ." (chapter 5); and now the image of "the Great Mother."

We are also told that what all three have in common is their "emptiness." The well is "used but never used up. It is like the eternal void." The bellows is "empty yet infinitely capable." And the Great Mother is "empty yet inexhaustible." It is this emptiness that makes them infinitely capable, inexhaustible, and capable of giving birth to infinite worlds. This theme of capability coming from emptiness is an important one, and we will return to it later.

Meanwhile what does all this mean to you? It means that because you are in the Tao and the Tao is within you, this potential emptiness with its accompanying capability is yours to use. The more you live in harmony with the Tao, the more empty you become and thus the more capability is at your command. "It is always present within you. You can use it any way you want."

The more you think about this idea, the more astonishing it becomes. Until you become aware that the act of thinking about it separates you from the Tao. Why? Because you become filled with thought instead of emptiness. Capability lies in emptiness. In fact, to the degree that you think about it, you are not dwelling in the Tao. You are separate from it.

When you dwell in harmony with the Tao, there is no thought and there is nothing to say. "The more you talk of it, the less you understand" (chapter 5). When you are centered in the Tao there is only emptiness and silence. If you dwell here, all your actions will be in natural harmony with the Tao and thus infinitely capable and inexhaustible. No thoughts. No words. Just dwelling, acting, and letting go.

How often we complicate our world with thoughts, words, and desires. And as a result, how full our finite worlds become. And yet the Tao is always there, present and inexhaustible. And we can step into the flow at any time.

Have you ever let go of your self and stepped into the flow? You may have done this either consciously or unconsciously. Children do it unconsciously all the time. As adults, however, we can do it on purpose. And when we do, we discover we can use the Tao "any way we want."

This chapter builds on the previous two. Not only is the Tao without limit and infinitely capable, it is also ours to use.

7

The Tao is infinite, eternal.
Why is it eternal?
It was never born;
thus it can never die.
Why is it infinite?
It has no desires for itself;
thus it is present for all beings.

The Master stays behind;
that is why she is ahead.
She is detached from all things;
that is why she is one with them.
Because she has let go of herself,
she is perfectly fulfilled.

The Tao has no desires.

This chapter explains how to dwell in the Tao. It starts by reminding us that the Tao is eternal because it exists outside time. The Tao was not "born" at some moment in the past and it will not "die" at some moment in the future. It simply is. If anything, it is eternally present. Always.

The text then goes on to observe that the Tao is "infinite." What's more, it explains why. "Why is it infinite? It has no desires for itself." Desire is what limits. And it limits because it makes distinctions. As soon as we desire, we distinguish what we desire from what we do not desire. We also distinguish ourselves from all other beings because they may or (more likely) may not desire whatever it is that we desire. Thus when we desire, we focus on ourselves. When we focus on ourselves, we separate ourselves from all other beings. When we are separate we cannot be fulfilled. This is neither good nor bad; it's just the way it is.

What's more, when we focus on our desires, we cease to live in the present moment. We are driven by our thoughts about some desired future state. We then look at the world not as it is but in terms of how it can help us achieve our goals. And we look at all beings in the same way. Thus, when we are driven by desire, we both focus on ourselves and live in the future. Contrast this with the Tao: "It has no desires for itself; thus it is present for all beings."

So what does the Master do? The answer is simple. She does not desire to be anywhere other than exactly where she is. You could say she is behind. You could say she is ahead. It doesn't matter which. You pick. Having no desires, she is not attached to them. Having no attachment, she is detached. Being detached, she is not separate from all things. Being not separate, "she is one with them." Being one with them, she is "perfectly fulfilled." This is what it means to dwell in the Tao.

How does the Master do this? Here comes the explanation: "Because she has let go of herself." Why is this significant? Because desire always springs from the "self" or, more strictly, the self-image, or ego. If you think about it, where else could it come from? And as soon as we have desire, we have everything else that goes with it, that is, attachment, separation, and lack of fulfillment. We may recall, "Free from desire, you realize the mystery. Caught in desire, you see only the manifestations" (chapter 1).

So the way to be perfectly fulfilled is to be one with all things, with no separation. The way to have no separation is to have no attachment. The way to have no attachment is to have no desire. The way to have no desire is to let go of your "self," which is the source of desire. When you let go of your self, you become empty. It is this emptiness that is the source of all capability and all fulfillment. This is how to dwell in the Tao. Note, there is no promise that any of this is easy. But it is simple.

How often we live caught in desire. We look to the future with fear and worry. Will our desires be fulfilled? We look back at the past with regret. What could we, or should we, have done so that our past desires would have been fulfilled and our present moment would therefore be somehow better? So many hypothetical versions of what might be! And every one of them draws us away from the present moment.

Have you ever looked at a situation and decided you didn't mind how it unfolded? Any way would have been fine. Have you noticed the freedom you feel when you do this? You have no attachment to one way or another. You are equally at peace with whatever happens. What if this could be true all the time?

This chapter reminds us that to desire is to become attached to the object of our desire. When we do this we see ourselves as separate. We mind very much how things unfold. We cling to our desired version of reality. To let go is to have no desire, no attachment. As a result there is no separation. This is where freedom and fulfillment lie. And yes, when you dwell in the Tao this is true all the time.

8

The supreme good is like water,
which nourishes all things without trying to.
It is content with the low places that people disdain.
Thus it is like the Tao.

In dwelling, live close to the ground.
In thinking, keep to the simple.
In conflict, be fair and generous.
In governing, don't try to control.
In work, do what you enjoy.
In family life, be completely present.

When you are content to be simply yourself
and don't compare or compete,
everybody will respect you.

How to live in the Tao.

Everything is in the Tao, of the Tao, and nourished by the Tao. In this respect it is like water. Water has no "desire." It is not "trying" to nourish anything. It just does what it does. It makes no judgments about high places and low places, thinking better of one and disdaining the other. Free from desire, we could say water is "content."

By the way, why are we ascribing thoughts and feelings to water? Good question. All we mean is that if you were like water in that you were free from desire, free from judgment, and content to nourish all things around you, then you would feel content. It's just an image.

So what words does the Master have for us to help us move in the world while dwelling in the Tao? What follows are six down-to-earth, practical recommendations. Do you want to know how to live in harmony with the Tao? Then do the following six things with respect to dwelling, thinking, conflict, governing, work, and family life. That should cover it for now.

Note that we have used the word "recommendations" because you have to choose to do these things for yourself. The Master cannot force you. As we saw earlier, the Master would in fact prefer to teach without saying anything, but if he resorted to words, then he certainly would not call them "commandments" or "laws." More likely he would pick a neutral word like "observations." Commandments and laws imply control, and the Master never tries to control you.

In dwelling, if you live close to the ground, then you haven't built some complicated structure. Simple is good. The same applies to your thinking. Keep it simple. It is inevitable that sooner or later there will be conflict. This is neither good nor bad. If anything, it is an opportunity not to think of yourself but to think of others. So be fair and generous to those with whom you are in conflict.

To control is to force things or people to be or act in a certain way. This is the expression of desire. Free from desire, you no longer need people to act in a certain way, so you no longer need to control. If your work calls for governing, then don't try to control.

Of course, you have to work in this human life. You may dwell in the Tao, but you are also moving in this world. To move in the world is to live. To live you need to act in harmony with the Tao to make a living. So what should your work be? Well, you have natural talents. You will recognize them because when you discover, develop, and apply them you will find you enjoy what you do. It will feel completely natural. Thus, as far as you are able, "in work, do what you enjoy." (Note that this is profoundly different from making yourself busy doing things to inflate your self-image in the eyes of others.)

When you work, be completely present in your work. When you stop work and are with your family, be completely present with them. Wherever you are, be completely there. Do not be distracted. Live completely in the present moment and you will dwell in harmony with the Tao.

In short, just be yourself. Don't compare yourself with others and desire to be like them. Don't compete with others to prove your superiority. Your self-image (or ego) exists only in relation to other people. So let it go. You are who you are. Be content "to be simply yourself." Paradoxically, by not striving to be respected by others, you will find they will respect you, for what this is worth. It will follow as a natural consequence. But it is not something to strive for.

How often we make life complicated. How seldom it needs to be this way. We tell ourselves we should "keep it simple," but this seems so difficult to do. What exactly does keeping it simple look like in practical, everyday terms?

Have you ever decided to uncomplicate your life but not known where to start? Or made a start and then wondered whether you should have started somewhere else?

This chapter reminds us that there are really only six areas to pay attention to. And none of them are complicated. Nor is what you need to do if you want to dwell in the Tao. It is all much simpler than we think. Maybe we sometimes make things needlessly complicated to avoid taking action. Hmm, there's a challenging thought.

Fill your bowl to the brim
and it will spill.
Keep sharpening your knife
and it will blunt.
Chase after money and security
and your heart will never unclench.
Care about people's approval
and you will be their prisoner.

Do your work, then step back.
The only path to serenity.

Do your work, then let go.

To dwell in the Tao is to let go of trying to possess things. Three types of things, to be specific: excessive material objects; abstract concepts relating to your personal future; and finally anything to do with your self-image, that is, what you think others think of you.

We know you cannot move in this world without using material objects. Of course you need food, water, shelter, and the like. However, most likely you don't need whatever your idea may be of "enough" of them. "Fill your bowl to the brim and it will spill." Whatever spills, you no longer possess. So you didn't need to fill "your bowl" to the brim. Less would be enough.

All material things are subject to change, so you cannot really possess any of them. "Keep sharpening your knife and it will blunt." Of course a knife that is not sharp is not much use. But don't expect that you can keep it sharp forever. Again, what matters is that it's sharp enough.

Second, striving to possess abstract things such as money or security can become a serious distraction, because you cannot hold on to them. If you try, "your heart will never unclench." You will find yourself caught up in the endless pursuit of money and security and will spend your life worrying about the future instead of living in the present. Again, what matters is knowing when to stop. Of course you need "enough." The trouble starts when you "chase after" more.

However, the third is the most important. We have already seen what happens when what you say and do becomes motivated by your self-image, or ego, that is, what you think others will think of you. "If you overesteem great men, people become powerless" (chapter 3). Chapter 9 elaborates on this idea by spelling it out in no uncertain terms. Not only do you become powerless, but "care about people's approval and you will be their prisoner." Strong words.

Why is this so important? Let's explore. You "are" what you think, say, and do. The question is, what motivates you, what is your intention? Your motivation can come from one of two places: your true inner self; or your external self-image, or ego. When what you think, say, and do springs from your true self, you are not trying to impress anybody. You would do the same even if nobody was watching. This is to move in harmony with the Tao.

However, when you are motivated by your self-image, or ego, you say and do things to earn the approval of others. What others think of you is what matters. When this is true in its extreme, you will stop at nothing to earn their approval. You will then, in effect, be their prisoner, because they will be able to control you by withholding or granting their approval. You will be like a puppet on a string. Live this way and you will never know peace, tranquility, and serenity. This is not dwelling in the Tao at all. The point is that the choice is yours.

To dwell in the Tao is to do your work simply for its own sake. The approval of others is irrelevant. Maybe they approve, maybe they don't. It doesn't matter. Their approval or disapproval certainly doesn't affect you, because your actions spring from your true self, not your self-image. This distinction is critical, because it's the difference between dwelling in the Tao and not dwelling in the Tao. It's the difference between conflict and harmony, between endless striving and serenity.

So the Master tells us, "Do your work, then step back," that is, with no attachment to the possible approval or disapproval of others. Is there any other way to dwell in the Tao? The answer is no. This is "the only path to serenity."

How often we desire particular outcomes as the result of our actions. When we do, the last thing we do is step back. Instead, we stay very close by in case things don't turn out exactly as we want. After all, we need to be ready to jump in and get things back onto the desired track. And how often do we "chase after" more? Money and security are good examples, but they're not the only ones. And how often do we care about other people's approval? Probably far more often that we'd like to admit.

And what happens when we do? In effect, we become the prisoner of our desire for the details of the outcome. Did our actions have the effect on others that we wanted? Did we earn enough money? Have we achieved enough security? (As though the answer to the last two questions could ever be yes.)

Have you ever done your work just for its own sake? Simply lost yourself in it. Just done what felt right at the time until you knew you were done. And then let go with no attachment to particular results.

This chapter reminds us what "stepping back" looks like. What do we experience when we do this? Serenity.

10

Can you coax your mind from its wandering
and keep to the original oneness?
Can you let your body become
supple as a newborn child's?
Can you cleanse your inner vision
until you see nothing but the light?
Can you love people and lead them
without imposing your will?
Can you deal with the most vital matters
by letting events take their course?
Can you step back from your own mind
and thus understand all things?

Giving birth and nourishing,
having without possessing,
acting with no expectations,
leading and not trying to control:
this is the supreme virtue.

Unchecked, our self will run the show.

The bottom line of this chapter is that you will never understand the Tao with your mind. The only way is to "step back from your own mind and thus understand all things." This is, of course, quite a blow to the machinery of thought of which we are generally so proud.

The first part spells out this idea in more detail by referring to five aspects of daily living: our mind, our body, our inner vision, loving people, and dealing with vital matters. These are pretty down-to-earth topics and a reminder that these writings are essentially a practical guide, not a theoretical treatise.

The common theme is self-discipline. Keeping yourself aligned with the Tao requires constant awareness. Unchecked, your mind will wander. You need to "coax" it back to the original oneness. Unchecked, your body will become rigid. You need to "let" it return to its natural state, supple as a newborn child's. Unchecked, your inner vision will become cloudy and dark with thoughts. You need to "cleanse" it until you see nothing but the light of emptiness. Otherwise you will remain trapped in your thoughts, a prisoner of your desire to have things be a certain way, and you will never dwell in the freedom of living in the Tao.

Let's continue. Unchecked, your actions with other people will tend to be attempts to impose your will on them. You need to love them and lead them without doing this. Unchecked, in daily affairs you will similarly try to impose your will. You need to let events take their course. Unchecked, you will dwell inside your own mind. If you do, you will never understand all things. You will always remain separate from the Tao and not part of the "original oneness."

What is it then to dwell in the Tao? What does it look like? Note that what follows is a description of simply "being." None of it describes a goal or an end-state or a destination. For example, it is not succeeding in securing possessions. It is simply having. It is not fulfilling a particular predetermined expectation. It is simply acting. It is not having finally got others under your control. It is simply leading, in whatever way is called for as "events take their course." It is giving birth and nourishing: "this is the supreme virtue."

This is hard stuff. Why? I think it's because our society admires those who strive for and achieve goals. Having lots of people under your control from your spot at the top of an organizational hierarchy is seen as the pinnacle of professional achievement. What's more, our society typically values material possessions as external indicators of success. Small wonder, then, that we tend to strive, control, and possess. Yet each one of these activities reinforces the separateness of where we are from where we want to be. What's more, we will never get there because we will never have enough. We will remain trapped in the rat race, constantly striving for "more."

In the Tao, there is no "there" to get to. We are already there. There is no striving to be done, no possessions to be secured, no control over others to be exerted, no "more" to be had. But does this mean we "do" nothing? Without goals, are our lives pointless? Absolutely not.

The point is not to "do things" dictated by the machinery of thought and the desires of our self-image. It is to "act" without attachment to an expected result, without seeking to control. To act with detachment, if you like. But we still care, even as we let "events take their course." We simply act with compassion and let go. To do this is to dwell in the Tao. When we dwell in the Tao, then harmony results and all manner of conflict and difficulty disappear. Is this easy? No. Is it worth it? Yes.

How often we let our minds take us wherever they want to go. Our "inner vision" becomes full of whatever our minds choose to think about—typically, desires and expectations of one sort or another. Whatever they are, you can be sure they're not part of the "original oneness." And then the trouble starts, because as soon as the thoughts are there, we start to act on them. Our minds insist: How can we achieve our goals without imposing our will? What guarantee will we have if we let events take their course? And so our minds try to run the show and control all the details.

Have you ever simply acted without desiring a particular result? This is not the same as acting "thoughtlessly." Rather it is like acting from "beyond thought," as it were. From this place, aware of how events are "taking their course," you simply act with compassion and let go. Shaping the flow. Leading without trying to control.

This chapter reminds us that doing so is the "supreme virtue."

11

We join spokes together in a wheel,
but it is the center hole
that makes the wagon move.

We shape clay into a pot,
but it is the emptiness inside
that holds whatever we want.

We hammer wood for a house,
but it is the inner space
that makes it livable.

We work with being,
but non-being is what we use.

Capability comes from emptiness.

We may recall, "The Tao is called the Great Mother: empty yet inexhaustible, it gives birth to infinite worlds" (chapter 6). This chapter explores this idea of emptiness with three metaphors.

The capability of the wheel to make the wagon move comes not from the spokes in the wheel but from the emptiness of the center hole. The capability of the pot to hold whatever we want to put in it comes not from the shaped clay but from the emptiness inside it. The capability of a house to be fit for living in comes not from the hammered wood but from the emptiness of the space within.

A wheel with no center hole would be useless. So would be a pot that was solid clay. So would be a house that was solid wood. And so it is with us. Our capability lies in being empty, not in being full. "We work with being, but non-being is what we use."

What is meant by "non-being"? Non-being is what's there when we let go of our self-image and allow our actions to spring from our true inner self. Unchecked, our self-image will use our actions to inflate itself in the eyes of others. When we are full of our self-image, our true self can never shine through. We are like the solid clay pot. Useless. It is in this respect that non-being is "emptiness."

What exactly is it that we need to be empty of? In a word, desire. If our mind is full of desires, then we see everything in terms of what we want it to be, not in terms of what it is. This chapter builds directly on the last one, where we saw how actions that spring from a mind full of desires will never be in harmony with the Tao. We will always try to control. We will try to impose our will. We will be driven by a desired future and so will fail to live in the present moment.

Why is this? It is because the mind abhors what it sees as the vacuum of emptiness. Left unchecked, it will fill itself with thoughts and desires. It will create imaginary future states in which it is better off because it has more possessions, more money, or more security or thinks it is held in higher esteem by others. Left unchecked, it will then direct our actions and use them as a means to an end. Conflict and difficulty will result. Harmony will be lost. Needless to say, we will not be dwelling in the Tao.

So how do we use "non-being" to dwell in the Tao? How do we check our mind, as it were? The answers lie in the previous chapter: "Coax your mind from its wandering." "Cleanse your inner vision until you see nothing but the light." "Love people and lead them without imposing your will." "Deal with the most vital matters by letting events take their course." Act "with no expectations . . . not trying to control" (chapter 10). This is what it means to be empty. It is from this emptiness that capability springs.

How often we act when we are full of ourselves. When we are like this, we are like a solid wheel, a solid clay pot, or a house with no space inside. All we're interested in is how to impose our will, how to get the results we want. Like this we are useless, at least in terms of living in harmony with the Tao.

Have you ever been frustrated that your best-laid plans just don't seem to be working out? The world just won't bend itself to your wishes. Of course, we usually don't see it that way. We don't feel we are imposing our will at all. We simply think we know best. We think we have everyone's best interests at heart. Or, more accurately, we have our idea of everyone's best interests at heart. And the world just doesn't seem to appreciate this "fact" and fall obediently in line. How frustrating.

This chapter reminds us that when we feel like this, we are not listening to the Tao. We are listening to our self. And the reality is that we become full of whatever we listen to. Listen to our self and we become full of our self. Listen to the Tao and we become empty of our self. It is from this emptiness that capability springs. Only then will our actions be in harmony with the Tao. Our actions will seem effortless. The wagon will roll without friction. The pot will hold whatever we like. The house will be the perfect place to dwell.

12

Colors blind the eye.
Sounds deafen the ear.
Flavors numb the taste.
Thoughts weaken the mind.
Desires wither the heart.

The Master observes the world
but trusts his inner vision.
He allows things to come and go.
His heart is open as the sky.

Trust and be open.

You cannot always trust your senses. They can give you too much misleading information. This is because they are plugged into the external world. And the external world is not the place from which to take direction. Thus your senses are important, but they are not to be trusted as a source of direction.

How true are the first few lines with respect to our busy world today. We experience constant assaults on our eyeballs with advertising that urges us to buy "things"; constant sounds in our ears with traffic, television, radio, cell phones, e-mail, and noise from the Internet; and constant varieties of flavors, each one supposedly better, newer, fresher, or more subtle than the last. It never ends. We become blinded, deafened, and numbed.

It is similar within ourselves. Our heads spin with too many thoughts. Our hearts are pulled this way and that by too many desires. Our minds become weakened and our hearts wither inside us. The result is that we become trapped, closed, and shut in.

What are we to do? Where do we place our trust? Let's see what the Master does.

For a start, the Master doesn't ignore what his senses tell him. But he doesn't take direction from it either. Instead he regards it neutrally. He "observes" it. This is a smart move. What is it that he does trust? His "inner vision." This is what guides his actions. This is how he moves in the world while dwelling in the Tao. What does guided action look like? Well, it is not driven by desire for things or people to be a certain way. Instead, the Master simply "allows things to come and go."

We may recall the same idea from earlier chapters. For example, "Things arise and she lets them come; things disappear and she lets them go" (chapter 2); "Don't try to control" (chapter 8); the Master deals with the most vital matters by "letting events take their course" (chapter 10). In a nutshell, the Master trusts his inner vision. He doesn't seek to control the external world by making it conform to his desires. And what is the result? Freedom and openness.

The point is, we have a choice. We can allow ourselves to be swamped with sensory information and be prisoners of our desire to control. In this case we will be trapped, closed, and shut in. Or we can let go of desire, in which case we will be free and "open as the sky." The choice is ours every moment of every day.

But, you may ask, if our actions are not guided by desires, then what guides them? In our freedom and our openness, from where does direction come? Good questions. They will be addressed in later chapters. For now, it is enough to understand these ideas of trust and openness, and choice.

How often we do the opposite of trusting. After all, how can we possibly fulfill our desires if we merely allow things "to come and go"? Surely we need to control them. And what is it that we desire anyway? So many choices of colors, sounds, flavors, and all the thoughts that go with them.

Have you ever chased after the latest version of something? Fallen prey to the marketing hype about the features of the latest model of some object or another? When you take direction from the marketing industry, you can be sure you will never be satisfied. In fact, the commercial world has a vested interest in ensuring that you're not satisfied, because if you were, they'd be out of business.

This chapter reminds us to observe the world but be careful not to take direction from it. What we should trust is our inner vision. When our interest is no longer vested in fulfilling our desires, we can let things come and go. Anything is possible. The sky is the limit.

————————— 13 —————————

Success is as dangerous as failure.
Hope is as hollow as fear.

What does it mean that success is as dangerous as failure?
Whether you go up the ladder or down it,
your position is shaky.
When you stand with your two feet on the ground,
you will always keep your balance.

What does it mean that hope is as hollow as fear?
Hope and fear are both phantoms
that arise from thinking of the self.
When we don't see the self as self,
what do we have to fear?

See the world as your self.
Have faith in the way things are.
Love the world as your self;
then you can care for all things.

Have faith in the way things are.

Why should both success and failure be equally dangerous? We might think success is "good" and failure is "bad." However, the problem lies neither in success nor in failure. It lies in two other places. First, in the fact that we think about them at all. Second, in the fact that we go on to make judgments about them and then start to hope for one and fear the other.

If you like, success is like a ladder. To go up the ladder is success and is to be hoped for. To go down is failure and is to be feared. The problem is the "ladder," because it will always be planted on the shaky ground of opinion—usually the opinion of others. Why? Because we usually define success and failure in terms of what others think. What they think of us determines our self-image. So if we take direction from our self-image, then we become prisoners not only of what others regard as "success" and "failure" but also of hope and fear.

The point is that we don't have to live this way. We can choose instead to take direction from within and be guided by our inner self. When we do this, what others think of us becomes irrelevant. We are not on the ladder. There is no up and no down. In fact there is no ladder. We are standing with our "two feet on the ground." We are who we are. What's more, we are balanced, because there is nothing to hope for and nothing to fear. "Hope and fear are both phantoms." "Phantom" is a great word to describe something that's not real. There's nothing real about hope and fear. They're completely artificial. They are manufactured by the machinery of thought. Once again our hyperactive minds are busy causing trouble.

It's worth exploring how this works. The trouble comes when we forget who we are (our true inner self), focus instead on our self-image, and then make the mistake of thinking that our self-image is who we really are. We do this in three steps. First, instead of just being our true inner self, we imagine the "self" that others see. (Strictly speaking, we imagine the self that we *think* others see.) Second, we then wonder whether others think this self is succeeding or failing. Third, we begin to hope for the former and fear the latter. We are on the ladder and so on shaky ground, all because we are caring about our self-image, which is an artifact of our mind.

The alternative is simple. We refrain from splitting ourselves into self and self-image and then becoming confused into thinking we "are" our self-image. Hope and fear then evaporate. "When we don't see the self as self, what do we have to fear?" The ladder just disappeared and our own feet are on solid ground. Is this magic? Not really. Just the result of choice. You can be separate from the Tao or you can step into it. Step into it and your self-image disappears, and so do all manner of conflict and difficulty, along with hope and fear.

So what does the Master recommend? Don't focus on your self. Focus on the world. Imagine there is no separation (because in fact there is no separation) except in your own mind. "See the world as your self." "Love the world as your self." Don't think you know better and that things "ought" to be a certain way, or that some ways are to be hoped for and others are to be feared. "Have faith in the way things are." Step into the Tao.

And what happens when you do? Then, no longer caring about your self-image, you become free and "you can care for all things." There is no separation between self, self-image, and world. Only unity. You are a part of everything and every thing is a part of you. Everything else is illusion. You "are" the world. Thus to love the world is to love your self. This is to dwell in the Tao.

How often we live on the ladder. Our organizations are full of ladders. We talk about promotion and demotion and being surpassed by others promoted over our heads. We look at one another's accumulations of possessions and judge who has more and fewer. More possessions and up the ladder are to be hoped for. Fewer of possessions and down the ladder are to be feared. No wonder our position is shaky.

Have you ever wondered what we mean when we say someone is "grounded" or "down-to-earth"? We mean their two feet are on the ground. They are not easily swayed by the opinions of others. They follow their true inner self. In the words of the last chapter, what they trust is their "inner vision."

This chapter reminds us that when we have faith in the way things are, we are on solid ground. We do not selectively hope for some things and fear others. We live phantom-free and "can care for all things."

Look, and it can't be seen.
Listen, and it can't be heard.
Reach, and it can't be grasped.

Above, it isn't bright.
Below, it isn't dark.
Seamless, unnamable,
it returns to the realm of nothing.
Form that includes all forms,
image without an image,
subtle, beyond all conception.

Approach it and there is no beginning;
follow it and there is no end.
You can't know it, but you can be it,
at ease in your own life.
Just realize where you come from:
this is the essence of wisdom.

The Tao is everything.

The Tao is everything. You can't split it up into separate things that you can look at, listen to, reach for, and grasp. It's not only everything, it's every thing, if you like. All of them. All at once. All together. Including you.

Because you can't split it up, you cannot name it. Because you cannot name it, you cannot describe it or talk about it. Let's see what happens when we try. "Above, it isn't bright. Below, it isn't dark." (It's a bit like a riddle.) "Bright" and "dark" don't work. Actually, nor do "above" and "below." It is all of them or none of them. Words work only when everything is split up into particular things that can be named. The Tao cannot be split up. If we have to use words, then "seamless" is a good one. So is "unnamable."

Being everything, the Tao consists of no "things." This means it has no convenient place in the realm of thought. "It returns to the realm of nothing." If we want to think of it as having a form, then it is the form that includes all particular forms. If we want to think of it as having an image, then it is the image without a particular image. Do you see how our minds struggle as the words fail?

Let's try some more words. "Approach it and there is no beginning; follow it and there is no end." "Beginning" and "end" don't work. Actually, nor do "approach" and "follow." We have the same problem as before. The Tao is all of them or none of them. If we have to pick words, then the phrase "subtle, beyond all conception" is good. Why? Because it puts the Tao safely beyond our knowledge and understanding. So these words work. As do "seamless" and "unnamable."

The trouble is that we cannot know and understand something that is seamless, unnamable, and subtle beyond all conception. Our minds cannot grasp it, precisely because it is not a "thing" or a "concept" that can conveniently be thought about. It is beyond knowing and understanding, which makes it a mystery. But it is only the mind that sees this as trouble. It isn't really. We just need to approach it in a different way. A mystery cannot be understood but it can nonetheless be "realized." Here's how:

Simply stop looking at the Tao as though it were something separate from you. Stop looking at yourself as though you were something separate from the Tao. Just as you cannot see the Tao, you cannot see your self. If you try, all you will see is your self-image, which is not real, because it's an artifact of your mind. It's an illusion. So shut down the machinery of thought. Step off the noisy treadmill in your mind and step into the Tao instead. Be quiet. Allow yourself to become it. Dwell in it. As the Master says, "You can't know it, but you can be it."

The moment you do this, the mental struggle will cease and you will live "at ease in your own life." Why? Because the truth is that you're not separate from the Tao. You never were. The struggle ceases as soon as you stop thinking that you are. "Just realize where you come from." You are not going anywhere. You're already there. As we saw in the last chapter, you are already a part of everything and every thing is already a part of you. Everything else is illusion.

All attempts to seek, know, and understand are part of the illusion. However, it is only your mind that will see this as trouble and be disappointed. And that's because you will no longer take your mind so seriously and let it control your life. The rest of you, as it were, will be able to live in harmony with the Tao and at ease in your own life. "This is the essence of wisdom." Your mind isn't useless, by the way. You just need to keep it in its place.

How often we struggle to put things into words. We want to understand and believe that finding the correct words is the way to do it. But it just doesn't work when we confront something as all-encompassing as the Tao. So what's the answer? The answer is not to confront the Tao or even try to wrap words around it. Why? Because all we need do is dwell in it.

Have you ever been "at ease in your own life"? No seeking. No questions. Just being. This is not passive, by the way. You are active, highly aware of the world around you, responding, acting, and letting go. But can you live in this state all the time? Yes.

This chapter reminds us that all we need to do is remember we come from the Tao, as does everything else. It can't be seen, it can't be heard, and it can't be grasped. But we don't need to understand the Tao to live in it. In fact, the less time we spend trying, the better.

The ancient Masters were profound and subtle.
Their wisdom was unfathomable.
There is no way to describe it;
all we can describe is their appearance.

They were careful
as someone crossing an iced-over stream.
Alert as a warrior in enemy territory.
Courteous as a guest.
Fluid as melting ice.
Shapable as a block of wood.
Receptive as a valley.
Clear as a glass of water.

Do you have the patience to wait
till your mud settles and the water is clear?
Can you remain unmoving
till the right action arises by itself?

The Master doesn't seek fulfillment.
Not seeking, not expecting,
she is present, and can welcome all things.

Be present and welcome all things.

We can learn what it's like to dwell in the Tao from the ancient Masters, who were really good at it. But we're going to quickly run up against the limitations of words. We could say the Masters were "profound," "subtle," and "unfathomable," but that doesn't really say a lot.

If we say more, we need to remember that any words we use to describe them will miss their true essence. This is because, like everything else, we cannot really split out and separate bits and pieces from the Tao. "All we can describe is their appearance." But describing appearances is a whole lot better than nothing. So let's try. What did the ancient Masters look like?

To dwell in the Tao is to be constantly aware of not letting your actions be controlled by your thoughts and desires. It is to constantly remember that only the Tao is real and that thoughts are illusions. So what does this look like? Well, as you move through life, it looks like being very careful that you don't fall through into the illusion of your thoughts. In this respect it's like walking on ice.

You could think of your thoughts and desires as waiting to pounce on you and control your actions. So dwelling in the Tao is like being constantly on guard against being taken over. You behave as if you were "in enemy territory."

To dwell in the Tao is to move in the world without making demands of it. "Courteous as a guest" describes it quite well. Here's another image: You are fluid, not solid. You do not try to bend the world out of shape to conform to your desires. You let it be. You are "shapable." You are open and receptive. Your mind is empty. A mind full of thoughts is like a glass of water full of particles. The minds of the ancient Masters would have been "clear as a glass of water."

So here's the challenge: Can you be like the Masters? Do you have the patience? Can you sit still enough for long enough?

I don't mean to be rude, but your mind is likely so full of thoughts that your glass is full of mud. So "do you have the patience to wait till your mud settles and the water is clear?" You're likely so used to moving in response to every thought, desire, and whim in your mind that you've forgotten how to be still. If you can be still, completely still, then you will find that the right action will arise all by itself. If you can succeed in this, you will no longer be controlled by your thoughts and emotions. Instead you will be moving in harmony with the Tao.

Desire always seeks to fulfill itself. You've got to get past this tendency (not that it's for me to tell you what to do), because desire causes endless seeking, endless expectations for things to be different in the future. The consequence is that you fail to live in the moment. To dwell in the Tao is to be here now.

So let's look at what the Master does. "She doesn't seek fulfillment." And what's the consequence? She doesn't live driven by some desired future state. She lives here and now, in the present moment. Because she is not closed to anything that doesn't help her fulfill her desires, she is able to be open, receptive, and accepting of everything. Instead of evaluating, judging, and accepting some things and rejecting others, "she is present, and can welcome all things."

Well, given the limitations of words, how did we do? Hopefully this description has helped a bit.

How often we lack patience. We are not present and we do not welcome all things. We are impatiently thinking about how to fulfill our desires and so live in an imaginary future. We believe the "right action" to take is the one that fulfills our desires, and that we need to figure out what that is. We believe that there's no way the right action would arise "all by itself." In the words of this chapter, our minds are full of mud.

Have you ever wondered what to do, gone to sleep at night, and then woken the next day with the answer, crystal clear? Where did it come from? As far as your mind is concerned, this right action did indeed arise all by itself. And it did that because your mind was unmoving while you slept. The mud had a chance to settle.

This chapter reminds us that we can choose to let the mud settle any time we want. All we need is patience. We can always see the right action when the water is clear.

---------------------------------- 16 ----------------------------------

Empty your mind of all thoughts.
Let your heart be at peace.
Watch the turmoil of beings,
but contemplate their return.

Each separate being in the universe
returns to the common source.
Returning to the source is serenity.

If you don't realize the source,
you stumble in confusion and sorrow.
When you realize where you come from,
you naturally become tolerant,
disinterested, amused,
kind-hearted as a grandmother,
dignified as a king.
Immersed in the wonder of the Tao,
you can deal with whatever life brings you,
and when death comes, you are ready.

Returning to the source is serenity.

Dwelling in the Tao and a mind full of thoughts just don't go together. The first line of this chapter makes this idea quite clear. So how do you get the thoughts out of your mind? Well, you don't think them out! The last chapter gave us one way: simply be patient and let them go. "Do you have the patience to wait till your mud settles and the water is clear?" (chapter 15).

What will you see once your mind is clear? You will see the "turmoil of beings" with much confusion and sorrow caused by people thinking their temporary separateness is all there is. This is what happens when we forget that apparent separateness is an illusion and that reality is unity. When our human lives are over, we go back to the reality we came from. We can't really talk about the afterlife (or heaven and hell and judgment, or whatever you want to call it), because we don't know what we're talking about. So let's just keep it simple and call it returning to the "common source" and leave it at that.

We all know our human life is temporary. But if we're not careful we spend much of our time driven by our thoughts and desires, all of which are based on splitting things up, separating them, naming them, making judgments about which are desirable or not, and pursuing those we think are desirable. No wonder we often "stumble in confusion and sorrow."

Why confusion? Because all aspects of separateness pull in the opposite direction of unity. So it's inevitable there will be confusion sooner or later. Why sorrow? Because desires often go unfulfilled. And when we pin happiness and sorrow on success and failure, then we are bound to get sorrow. And, depending on what we pin our happiness on, even happiness can be fleeting, especially if it's based on anything to do with possessions.

So what does the Master do? He dwells in the Tao by being constantly aware of the big picture. He doesn't pin anything anywhere. The reality is that you came here with nothing. You're going to leave with nothing. All you have in the meantime are your actions and a constant choice that you have to make. Are you going to dwell in the Tao or in the illusion of your thoughts and desires? Are you going to act with compassion guided by wisdom and let go of expectation? Or are you going to be driven by thought and desire and live in confusion and sorrow? You pick.

"Returning to the source is serenity." It's where you're headed anyway. So what happens if you live in constant awareness of this? For a start, you don't get attached to temporary distractions. You're "disinterested." You may watch the turmoil of beings, but you don't interfere. You remember not to judge, because to judge is to think, split, separate, and compare. The reality is that we're all here living our own temporary lives. Your way is no "better" than anyone else's. The least you can do is be "tolerant" and at most "amused." "Kind-hearted as a grandmother, dignified as a king." These words are a good description.

To dwell in the Tao is simply to immerse yourself in its wonder. No judging. No thinking. Just acting with compassion and letting go. If you live like this you won't get swept up in the turmoil. You will be able to "deal with whatever life brings you." Death will come sooner or later. It doesn't matter when, because you won't be full of hopes, fears, and regrets. You'll be ready.

How often we find ourselves caught up in the "turmoil of beings." How often we stumble in confusion and sorrow. Our default way of dealing with the world is to fill our minds with thoughts. If something isn't working out the way we want, we think: Why is that? What's going wrong? What do we need to do to fix it? Why doesn't this way or that way work? All these thoughts take us further and further away from the reality of what is. In the words of this chapter, we are not "tolerant," we are not "disinterested," and we are certainly not "amused."

Have you ever just taken a deep breath and emptied your mind? Just contemplated a situation for what it is, with no vested interest in having reality be your version of what it should be? What happens when we do this? In short, we let go. Our pulse rate drops, our heart is at peace. We become free to simply listen and respond in whatever way is called for by the natural flow of what's happening around us.

This chapter reminds us that the experience described above is what it's like when we return to the source. Centered in the reality of what is, instead of separated and lost in our own thoughts. This is where serenity lies.

17

When the Master governs, the people
are hardly aware that he exists.
Next best is a leader who is loved.
Next, one who is feared.
The worst is one who is despised.

If you don't trust the people,
you make them untrustworthy.

The Master doesn't talk, he acts.
When his work is done,
the people say, "Amazing:
we did it, all by ourselves!"

Trust others.

This chapter is about how to lead while acting in harmony with the Tao. Remember, "The Master acts without doing anything and teaches without saying anything" (chapter 2). This chapter spells out how dwelling in the Tao applies to leadership and government.

Here's the challenge: "Can you love people and lead them without imposing your will?" (chapter 10); and, "In governing, don't try to control" (chapter 8). Chapter 17 opens by describing what it looks like when you succeed in meeting this challenge. It looks as though you're invisible. This is as good as it gets. Why? Because you attract no personal attention. It's not about you and whether or not you're a great leader. It's about what happens when you act in a certain way.

If you act with intent to be seen as a great leader, then you will be trapped by the desire to inflate your self-image. You will see yourself not only as separate from the Tao, but also as separate from other leaders less "great" than you think you are. It will be all about you.

The next-best thing to as good as it gets is to be a leader who is loved. Why is this next best? Because attention is still attracted to you. In this case, you're a leader who is loved, which is certainly better than one who is feared or despised. But attention is attracted to you nonetheless, and dwelling in the Tao involves no thought of separateness. However, to be loved at least means people are likely to want to be governed by you. So they will follow willingly. If you like, they will follow with their hearts and minds.

Next best after being a leader who is loved is to be one who is feared. This is not so good, because (apart from attracting attention to yourself) people will not want to be governed by you but will fear feeling this way. So they will go along. But they will follow unwillingly. If you like, they will follow with their minds but not with their hearts.

Worst is to be a leader who is despised. Again, people are aware of you, but in this case they neither love nor fear nor respect you. They will ignore you or, if they comply with your governing, they will follow with neither their hearts nor their minds. This is definitely the worst.

Best is simply to dwell in the Tao and act in harmony with it. This does not call for thought at all. Instead, it calls for constant awareness of the Oneness/Wholeness of all things. As we've seen earlier, dwelling in the Tao calls for simply acting with compassion and letting go. The trouble with thought is that as soon as you let it direct your actions, you need to become very careful how you think. Why? Because thought will separate, divide, make distinctions, and then make judgments about the distinctions. If you're not careful, you will then find yourself acting as if the distinctions are real.

Do you remember how this works? "Being and non-being create each other." "When people see some things as good, other things become bad" (chapter 2). Here's what it looks like when this idea is applied to leadership. "If you don't trust the people, you make them untrustworthy." Isn't it interesting that *their* untrustworthiness is a consequence of *your* thought? Think differently and you'll get a different consequence. It's best, of course, not to take direction from "thought" at all.

This is what the Master does. He does not think or make distinctions and judgments and talk about them. He simply acts. He gets himself out of the way. This is why he attracts no attention to himself. This is why he's invisible. And what is the consequence? "When his work is done, the people say 'Amazing: we did it, all by ourselves!' Perfect.

How often we think it's all about us. What we do is all that matters. And if we are governing others, then what matters is that they do what we tell them. After all, we are the leader, so their job is to follow. Trusting people to do things all by themselves seems way too risky. After all, they may get it wrong.

Have you ever had a really good manager at work? It would have felt as though you weren't working for them, more as though you were working with them. They knew they were the boss, you knew they were the boss, but somehow it just didn't feel that way. And didn't you produce your best work under those conditions? Why was that? The answer is that they trusted you.

This chapter reminds us that bringing out the best in others is all about them, not about you. You may set a direction, but when it's time for action the best thing you can do is get out of the way. Experts in today's workplace call this "empowerment" and talk about not "micromanaging" others, but the idea has been around for a long time. It's called trust.

18

When the great Tao is forgotten,
goodness and piety appear.
When the body's intelligence declines,
cleverness and knowledge step forth.
When there is no peace in the family,
filial piety begins.
When the country falls into chaos,
patriotism is born.

Remember the Tao.

To dwell in the Tao is to be constantly aware of the big picture. When you do not dwell in the Tao you are unaware of the whole picture. Instead, all you see are the pieces of the picture. "Goodness" and "piety" are pieces, because they are the products of thought. Do you remember, "When people see some things as beautiful, other things become ugly. When people see some things as good, other things become bad" (chapter 2)? The idea here is the same. It all has to do with our tendency to see "things," separate them, and name them.

When you dwell in the Tao your actions are in natural harmony with it. There is no need to label your actions "good" or to label yourself as "pious." These are artificial distinctions. You are just dwelling, acting, and letting go. No labels are required. It is only "when the great Tao is forgotten" that "goodness and piety appear."

If you can bring yourself to disconnect from the machinery of thought, you will make an interesting discovery. The "body's intelligence" will take care of you, all on its own. You just have to trust it. The question is, can you let your mind be quiet? Can you remain unmoved by wherever your latest thoughts take you? "Can you remain unmoving till the right action arises by itself?" (chapter 15). A lot of the time the answer is no. And whenever that's the case, then "cleverness and knowledge step forth"; the mind is in charge, thought is king, and awareness of the Tao is nowhere in sight.

This state of being occurs because thought always separates the big picture into distinguishable pieces. It's very clever that way. In contrast, dwelling in the Tao has nothing to do with distinctions or with cleverness or knowledge. Instead, it has everything to do with Oneness/Wholeness. Awareness of this truth is what brings peace—peace that literally "passes all understanding" (to borrow a quote from another context).

When there is no peace, we live among the pieces, if you will pardon the pun. "When there is no peace in the family, filial piety begins." "Filial piety" is like "goodness" in the first line. It's a piece. Similarly, when a country is at peace, there is no need to distinguish it as an entity to feel patriotic about. It is only when "the country falls into chaos" that "patriotism is born." Patriotism is another piece. It's all about identifying with one country as opposed to another. It's about "my" country as opposed to "your" country. Patriotism thrives, as it were, on distinctions and attaches importance to differences. It couldn't exist unless we distinguished one country from another. In this respect, patriotism is a typical thought in that it focuses on differences, distinctions, and separateness.

What do these "pieces" all have in common? They are all the result of forgetting the Tao. Dwell in the Tao and there will be peace in the family and in the country. When there is peace there is no need for filial piety and patriotism. There is also no need for cleverness and knowledge, for that matter. Here is another blow to the machinery of thought.

A self-important mind won't find that a tasty idea to chew on for any length of time!

How often we hold cleverness and knowledge in high esteem. We admire depth of knowledge and look down on shallow knowledge. More knowledge always seems to be a good thing.

You've likely heard the paradoxical phrase "less is more." What if we applied this idea to cleverness and knowledge? Doing so goes against the grain, doesn't it? But if we look closely, we don't actually need "less," we simply need to keep what we have in its place. The trouble starts only when cleverness and knowledge step forth. And that happens only when "the great Tao is forgotten." That is when confusion and chaos begin.

This chapter reminds us to remember the Tao. When we focus on Oneness/Wholeness, we rise above distinctions and all the potential chaos that goes with them.

19

Throw away holiness and wisdom,
and people will be a hundred times happier.
Throw away morality and justice,
and people will do the right thing.
Throw away industry and profit,
and there won't be any thieves.

If these three aren't enough,
just stay at the center of the circle
and let all things take their course.

Stay at the center of the circle.

This is a continuation of the list we started in chapter 18, of all the separate pieces that appear when we forget the Oneness/Wholeness that is the Tao. In chapter 18, we had goodness, piety, cleverness, knowledge, and patriotism. In this chapter, we add holiness, wisdom, morality, justice, industry, and profit. This is an interesting exercise because, at first glance, how could we think that holiness, wisdom, morality, and justice should be "thrown away"? Surely they should be venerated and aspired to. Whatever's wrong with them?

This is exactly where the Master wants our mind to be. Why? Because now we are ready to push on through to what's there on the other side of thought. To which the answer is "nothing." Just peaceful dwelling in the Tao with none of these labels. Just emptiness and silence. Needless to say, our minds find this concept hard to deal with. We don't trust it. It seems too simple. Surely it's more complicated than that.

The basic question is, why do we trust our minds so much more than what chapter 18 called "the body's intelligence"? It's our mind that distinguishes holiness, wisdom, morality, and justice. And in doing so it causes all of their opposites to spring into being. We then go on to make all sorts of judgments about how the first are better than the latter. And we make judgments that people who live according to the first are good and those who do not are bad—that they are "thieves," for example. This process is the slippery slope of thought in action. Where to next? Maybe we should feel justified in punishing thieves. But, wait a moment, do you think thieves think of themselves as thieves? What if they don't? Is "thievery" in the eye of the beholder? There we go. Now we've succeeded in making things nice and complicated. Thought is at it again.

What would happen if we were to throw away all these distinctions? What if we were to shut down the machinery of thought and simply trust our inner selves to live in harmony with the Tao? Here's what will happen. "People will be a hundred times happier." "People will do the right thing." "There won't be any thieves." Really? Do we honestly think that? The truth is, we likely don't. We likely think we need the concepts of morality and justice or everything will fall into chaos, which, of course, means we need the machinery of thought that distinguishes them in the first place. And there's precisely the trouble! It's all this thinking, which includes thought justifying itself.

What would happen if we called its bluff? Have you ever tried to think about not thinking? It can't be done. If you succeed, then you're thinking. It's the trying that will trap you. To succeed, the only thing you can do is throw thought away. Just stop thinking. Step out of the noisy machinery of your mind and step into the quiet, flowing waters of the Tao.

Doing this is not easy. Letting go is hard to do. And if you think about it, it becomes very hard indeed. How can we not think? One way that might help is to stop thinking in terms of opposites, for example, good and bad or right and wrong. Instead of polar opposites at each end of straight line, think of these concepts as arranged along the rim of a circle. Are any of them now any "better" than any others? It's harder to make a judgment now. So don't try. Simply stop thinking about it. Just "stay at the center of the circle."

Similarly, don't try to interfere. Just "let all things take their course." Do you really think you know any better? If so, then question your "thinking" and your "knowledge." Then when you're done questioning them, don't make any judgments, just let them go and trust yourself to the Tao.

How often we spend time at the outer edge of the circle making finer and finer distinctions between subtle details of abstract concepts like morality and justice. And how often we think we know better than to let things take their course.

Have you ever wondered whether this time at the outer edge of the circle is time well spent? Sometimes it is. But is it the best basis for action all the time? Not really. Often we simply know what to do. In fact, have you ever caught yourself using thought and analysis to justify your actions in hindsight? Thought just doesn't want to be left out of the picture, does it?

This chapter reminds us to throw away abstract concepts and ulterior motives, stay at the center of the circle, and trust ourselves to the Tao.

20

Stop thinking, and end your problems.
What difference between yes and no?
What difference between success and failure?
Must you value what others value,
avoid what others avoid?
How ridiculous!

Other people are excited,
as though they were at a parade.
I alone don't care,
I alone am expressionless,
like an infant before it can smile.

Other people have what they need;
I alone possess nothing.
I alone drift about,
like someone without a home.
I am like an idiot, my mind is so empty.

Other people are bright;
I alone am dark.
Other people are sharp;
I alone am dull.
Other people have a purpose;
I alone don't know.
I drift like a wave on the ocean,
I blow as aimless as the wind.

I am different from ordinary people.
I drink from the Great Mother's breasts.

Do not be guided by others.

Thought is the root of all problems. This is because it splits, separates, and makes distinctions. The danger lies in the distinctions. Yes and no, success and failure. The particular examples don't matter. The problem is always the same. Do you remember the observation "Success is as dangerous as failure" (chapter 13)? The idea here is the same.

Why the "danger"? Because we don't stop at making distinctions. We go on to make judgments about concepts like success and failure and then let our judgments determine what we value or don't value, what we do or don't do, what we move toward or avoid. Let's stop and think about this for a moment. It's strange, isn't it? "Must you value what others value, avoid what others avoid?" Do you really have to look to others to take direction for your own actions? "How ridiculous!"

In what follows, the Master describes what he looks like when compared with someone who is not dwelling in the Tao, that is, with someone who is unaware, who is living in the "ordinary" world. His description shows what happens when we use the machinery of thought to make those distinctions of which we are so fond. As a result, the words are tongue in cheek, as we shall see.

Other people at a parade get excited. There is something to look at, something to talk about, have an opinion about, or make a comment on. "I alone don't care. I alone am expressionless." Note that the Master is not saying there's anything wrong with the parade. He's just saying he has nothing to say about it. He has no opinion. Nothing to say. Do you know what a baby looks like before it has learned how to express happiness or sadness? The master is like that, "like an infant before it can smile." Neither good nor bad. No comment. Other people have possessions and attach importance to them, which gives those people direction. Their minds are full of thoughts and knowledge. "I alone possess nothing. I alone drift about, like someone without a home. I am like an idiot, my mind is so empty."

Why are these words said tongue in cheek? Because the Master, dwelling in the Tao, is aware he is already "home" and that he doesn't need to possess anything. He understands the limitations of so-called "knowledge," so he keeps his mind as empty as possible of thoughts. Does this really make him an "idiot"? No, of course it doesn't.

The Master carries on. Compared with other people, he is "dark," "dull," without purpose. He is not driven by desire. Instead he appears to drift about "like a wave on the ocean." He is not goal-oriented in a particular direction. Instead it appears that he blows "as aimless as the wind." But is he really "drifting about"? No, of course not. He simply has no desire to be anywhere other than where he is. If others think he's drifting about, then, to use a current phrase, we could say that's their problem, not his.

The tongue comes out of the cheek in the last couple of lines. "I am different from ordinary people." (No kidding.) And here's the consequence: the Master, dwelling in harmony with the Tao, is at peace and is aware that he truly lacks nothing. He doesn't need possessions or what others would call a home, or goals or direction or brightness or sharpness or purpose or knowledge. He doesn't need to be anywhere other than where he is. He is aware that he is already part of the Tao, part of the Great Mother (remember chapter 6?). This means he doesn't need to strive to possess anything. He already has all he needs.

There is no need to strive to "drink from the Great Mother's breasts." She is always there. The truth is, you're already home. The milk is free.

How seldom we stop thinking. And as though that were not enough, we think about what we think others are thinking. Others value this or that; should we do so too?

Have you ever responded to peer pressure? Have you ever looked over your shoulder to see what others are looking at and how they're reacting to it? Have you ever wondered why you did that instead of just trusting yourself?

This chapter has one thing to say about taking direction from others: "How ridiculous!" That doesn't leave much to the imagination, does it?

21

The Master keeps her mind
always at one with the Tao;
that is what gives her her radiance.

The Tao is ungraspable.
How can her mind be at one with it?
Because she doesn't cling to ideas.

The Tao is dark and unfathomable.
How can she make it her radiant?
Because she lets it.

Since before time and space were,
the Tao is.
It is beyond *is* and *is not*.
How do I know this is true?
I look inside myself and see.

Stay at one with the Tao.

How does the mind help us dwell in the Tao? The answer is, not a lot. Unchecked, the mind will wander off and do its own thing. It will view and analyze the world. It will split, separate, and name the apparently different things it chooses to distinguish. It will then build structures of thought and knowledge to try to grasp what it thinks is reality. The mind generates lots of noise and activity. Does this help us dwell in the Tao? Not really.

Let's see what the Master does. She keeps her mind "at one with the Tao." This is easy to say, but just what does it mean? It means her mind does not try to grasp the Tao and pigeonhole it into a convenient slot in the structure of thought and knowledge. The Master knows that "the Tao is ungraspable." But then how can her mind be at one with it? That's a good question.

The answer is to stop attaching so much importance to thought, to stop building our favorite complicated structures of knowledge. All these do is separate us from the Tao. As long as we keep doing this, we will never be at one with it. The Master is aware of this truth, which is why "she doesn't cling to ideas." She knows they will always get in the way.

As we've seen before, ideas and thoughts can never fathom the Tao. The Tao is as "dark and unfathomable" as it is ungraspable. If thought is like a flashlight, you can shine it all you like at the Tao and you will never see anything. It's like aiming your flashlight at the dark side of the moon expecting to see it light up. There's not a chance that will work.

If you want to see the light, stop playing with the flashlight. That's not where the light comes from. It is the illusion that you're somehow separate from the Tao that keeps you in the dark. And the more you rely on the mind with its little flashlight, the darker everything will seem. If you can be quiet and simply let your mind at be one with the Tao, then it is as if magic happens. You'll find you don't need a light, because the light is already there. And when you dwell in the Tao, the light is in you. The Master knows this: "that is what gives her her radiance."

How does the Master dwell in the light? The answer is simple. She stops trying. Knowing the light is already there, she shuts off the flashlight of her mind. She doesn't try to "make" the Tao be her light. It's simpler than that: "she lets it." She surrenders to it, if you like. She embodies it. And as a result she shines in harmony with the Tao. She is radiant.

Remember how thought splits, separates, and divides into what "is" and what "is not"? The Tao is beyond all that—unfathomable, ungraspable. "It is beyond is and is not." It is beyond space and time and all the boundaries of thought. We could say it always was and always will be, but even that's speaking from within thought. The Tao simply "is."

How does the Master know this? Is it through intellectual effort? Do you need to analyze the Tao, study it, name the pieces, grasp them, fathom them, discuss them, and arrange them into elegant patterns? Is the Tao at the pinnacle of some complicated structure of knowledge? No. The Tao is not out there. You're facing the wrong way. Look inside. It's already there. You are a part of it. Everything is. As the Master says, "I look inside myself and see." End of story. And the beginning of serenity.

Just let your mind be quiet. Live in constant awareness. And you will dwell in harmony with the Tao. What's more, you will shine radiantly with it.

How often we cling to ideas. It seems we believe that with sufficient thought everything is fathomable. Maybe it is, maybe it isn't. But the question is, why do we need to fathom it? If the Tao is like a river and we live in its flow, does it matter how deep it is?

Have you ever met a "radiant" person? Maybe he or she was what others would call a religious or spiritual person, but maybe not. (As usual, the label adds little value.) They seem to move through life with a peace and serenity that you can feel when you're in their presence. This is the light shining. And how do they do that? The answer is, they simply let it.

This chapter reminds us that dwelling in the Tao is not about grasping ideas that are out there somewhere. It's about looking inside, discovering that the light is already there, and letting it shine.

22

If you want to become whole,
let yourself be partial.
If you want to become straight,
let yourself be crooked.
If you want to become full,
let yourself be empty.
If you want to be reborn,
let yourself die.
If you want to be given everything,
give everything up.

The Master, by residing in the Tao,
sets an example for all beings.
Because he doesn't display himself,
people can see his light.
Because he has nothing to prove,
people can trust his words.
Because he doesn't know who he is,
people recognize themselves in him.
Because he has no goal in mind,
everything he does succeeds.

When the ancient Masters said,
"If you want to be given everything,
give everything up,"
they weren't using empty phrases.
Only in being lived by the Tao
can you be truly yourself.

Let go of your self.

We constantly strive to fulfill our wants and desires, to become something we're not. As we have seen elsewhere, we will never succeed. The way to dwell in the Tao is not to "want" to become anything. Rather it is to "let" things unfold. To the goal-oriented person, striving to meet his or her objectives by prespecified deadlines, this all likely sounds rather pointless. As a matter of fact, it isn't. But before we go there, here's a practical tip to help you increase your self-awareness.

You have two choices. You can either be driven by wants or desires, which is to be closed, or be open to letting the Tao unfold through you. Here's how to tell the difference. As soon as you become aware of a "want," stop and make yourself open to its opposite. That doesn't mean you want the opposite. It simply means you become aware of your closed mind, become open to other possibilities, and, hopefully, become willing to let them unfold. The key word is "let." It is quite different from "want."

Here are some examples of this idea in action. Do you want to become whole? Let yourself be partial. Do you want to become straight? Let yourself be crooked. Full? Empty. Reborn? Die. Be given everything? Give up everything. Do you see how it works? The idea is to get to the other side of "want to become" and replace it with "let it unfold."

What are the results when we look at the Master "residing in the Tao"? He doesn't "want to become" anything. He simply resides. The result is that he "sets an example for all beings." He is not full of himself, driven by his self-image, desiring that others think well of him. When we are full of ourselves, we obscure the light of the Tao within us. When people look at the Master, he is empty of himself. The result is that "people can see his light."

The Master does not try to control others or assert himself or "prove" himself in the eyes of those around him. He is not motivated by self-interest. The result is that "people can trust his words." Because he is not full of himself and does not define his self-worth relative to others, we might think "he doesn't know who he is." The result is that he could be any person or every person. It doesn't matter. But "people recognize themselves in him." That does matter. Why? Because this is how he "sets an example for all beings."

In summary, the Master does not "want to become" anything. He is not driven by wants or desires. He is not goal-oriented, objective-driven, or deadline-conscious. He is certainly aware of his actions, but not in a conventional, premeditated way. It is precisely "because he has no goal in mind" that "everything he does succeeds."

This idea is paradoxical, isn't it? How can you succeed in achieving a goal you don't set? The answer is that you succeed because, contrary to what we think, success does not require goals. The Master does not "succeed" in dwelling in harmony with the Tao. He just does it and lets it be. I'm sure he would smile if we told him he was "succeeding." But note that his life is not passive and pointless. On the contrary, as we have seen, his actions can have profound results.

Only when you stop being driven by your goal-setting self-image can your true inner self shine through. Your inner self already lives in the Tao. The Tao already lives in you. You just need to let go and let it be. So instead of trying to live in the Tao "on purpose," as though it were a goal to be achieved, simply surrender. Be lived by the Tao, if you like. "Only in being lived by the Tao can you be truly yourself."

How often we try to prove who we are. We are driven by our self-image. When we do this we set ourselves apart from the Tao. We believe we need to be somebody or something we're not.

Have you ever wanted anything to be different about yourself? Examples in this chapter include whole, straight, and full. You could also add more beautiful, less heavy, physically stronger. It doesn't matter what. The point is, you're focusing on something that isn't the case. Your light is dimmed to the degree that you don't recognize it for what it already is.

This chapter reminds us that the way to dwell in the Tao is to let go of our self. When we do, our life flows without effort. We seem to succeed without trying, to be given everything we need without striving for it. This is what it's like when the light shines.

23

Express yourself completely,
then keep quiet.
Be like the forces of nature:
when it blows, there is only wind;
when it rains, there is only rain;
when the clouds pass, the sun shines through.

If you open yourself to the Tao,
you are at one with the Tao
and you can embody it completely.
If you open yourself to insight,
you are at one with insight,
and you can use it completely.
If you open yourself to loss,
you are at one with loss
and you can accept it completely.

Open yourself to the Tao,
then trust your natural responses;
and everything will fall into place.

Open yourself to the Tao.

To dwell in the Tao is to act, holding nothing back, and then to let go completely. This means letting go of a particular expected outcome, letting your mind become free from desire, emptying it of all noisy thoughts. "Express yourself completely, then keep quiet." This is not easy.

If you want a model, "Be like the forces of nature." Nature doesn't think; it just is. Nature makes no comment about what it does, as it were. It has no desires, no expectations from its actions. "When it blows, there is only wind; when it rains, there is only rain." The key word is "only." There is nothing else. Nature acts and lets go. It is beautiful in its simplicity. "When the clouds pass, the sun shines through." What could be simpler than that?

So why don't we act like this? The reason is that our minds tend to make things complicated. Unchecked, they are full of thoughts and closed to outcomes other than the ones we desire. We tend to see everything in terms of what we want it to be. We see possessions and other people as means to whatever end we have in mind at the time. When we are like this, we are full of ourselves. When we are full of ourselves, there is no room for the Tao. We will never be "at one" with it, in the present moment. We will always be separate.

The Master recommends the forces of nature as a role model because nature is always completely in the moment. Nothing is held back. Nothing is held onto. There is "only" wind or "only" rain. This is what happens to us when we open ourselves to the Tao. There is "only" the Tao and we are completely part of it. We embody it, if you like. "You are at one with the Tao and you can embody it completely." There is no separation.

The same idea applies to insight. Typically we are closed to insight because we are too busy looking outward at what we think is the external, separate world out there. "If you open yourself to insight, you are at one with insight and you can use it completely." We may recall, "The Tao . . . is always present within you. You can use it any way you want." (chapter 6). Capability comes from being "at one" with the Tao, being at one with insight, and trusting yourself to it.

And the same idea applies to feelings. Peace and serenity come from acceptance. Acceptance comes from being at one. Being at one comes from being open. For example, "If you open yourself to loss, you are at one with loss and you can accept it completely." Difficulty comes from being closed to loss, thereby keeping it separate and unacceptable.

All this is so simple to say but, typically, so difficult to do. Why? Because our minds get in the way with all their noisy thoughts and desires. We typically separate ourselves from the present moment; we desire particular outcomes in the future and use our present actions as a means to get them. We then usually also go on to spend a fair bit of time regretting the past and worrying about the future. All of which prevent us from living in the moment. We cannot be at one with the Tao, because we are too full of ourselves.

And yet the Tao is right in front of us all the time. All we have to do is let go, be open to it, and trust. We then "can embody it completely," "can use it completely," and "can accept it completely." What's called for is trust. "Trust your natural responses; and everything will fall into place."

How often we are closed. We see only what we want to see. We are on the inside looking out. How can we have "insights" this way? What are we having? "Outsights," perhaps? Insight comes only when we are open. What's more, it is not something we have. Rather it is something we become "at one with." Nature is such a good model because it is always at one with itself. If you think about it (which is not recommended), how could it be otherwise?

Have you ever walked among the big trees or along the sea shore and let your mind become quiet? Completely quiet. When your mind becomes quiet, you become open, at one with whatever is. You become aware of the wind, the rain, the clouds passing, the sun shining through—and nothing else. This is all you're aware of. It completely fills the moment.

This chapter reminds us that this experience is what it's like to be open. When you are open, there is no separation between you and insight, between you and your feelings, between you and the Tao. You are insight. You are your feelings. You are dwelling in the Tao. Trust the Tao, trust your natural responses, and "everything will fall into place." What could be simpler?

24

He who stands on tiptoe
doesn't stand firm.
He who rushes ahead
doesn't go far.
He who tries to shine
dims his own light.
He who defines himself
can't know who he really is.
He who has power over others
can't empower himself.
He who clings to his work
will create nothing that endures.

If you want to accord with the Tao,
just do your job, then let go.

Just do your job, then let go.

Dwelling in the Tao does not call for effort, or desire, or action intended to fulfill desire. If it calls for anything, then it calls for "letting go." To live in harmony with the Tao, "just do your job, then let go." Action intended to fulfill desire is at best limited and at worst backfires. Why? Because not only does the act of grasping fail to succeed in grasping, but what is grasped for also becomes further out of reach.

Six examples clarify this. "He who stands on tiptoe doesn't stand firm." Standing on tiptoe is a response to a desire to see farther, but the result is that you may lose your balance. "He who rushes ahead doesn't go far." Rushing ahead is a response to a desire to go farther or arrive sooner, but the result is that you don't go far.

The backfiring is particularly obvious when you act with intent to impress others. Attempts to inflate your self-image in the eyes of others are always at the expense of your true inner self. Why? Because whenever you become "full of yourself" there is no room for who you really are. Light comes from your true inner self. Thus "he who tries to shine dims his own light." The result is exactly the opposite of what is desired. Remember how it is with the Master? "Because he doesn't display himself, people can see his light" (chapter 22). The idea here is the same. In fact, to the degree you try to shine or try to display yourself, you dim your own light. The problem lies in the trying.

Three more examples follow. As we have seen earlier, thought and knowledge always call for distinction and definition. And with both of these invariably comes limitation. "He who defines himself can't know who he really is." In this case, defining yourself is a response to a desire to know who you really are; assuming a neat definition will allow you to pigeonhole yourself in the structure of knowledge. There are two problems with this. First, you will always be limited by your own definition. Second, knowing who you really are does not require the context of knowledge and definition in the first place. You already are who you are. What's called for is awareness, not knowledge.

Become preoccupied with your power over others and you will lose your own empowerment of yourself. Note that there is nothing wrong with power over others as long as you stay in harmony with the Tao. In fact, it is an awesome responsibility. We may recall, "When the Master governs, the people are hardly aware that he exists" (chapter 17). This is what governing in harmony with the Tao looks like. The problem lies in becoming preoccupied with power over others at the expense of how you handle yourself.

The final example is about acting with desire to achieve an expected outcome. Typically, we cling to "our" work. We want it to succeed by our standards. We may also want it to be noticed by others so they will think more highly of us as a result, thereby inflating our self-image. This is not the way to go. Whatever we produce by acting this way will never last. "He who clings to his work will create nothing that endures." The problem lies in the clinging.

So what are the solutions? The same solution applies to all six examples. It is simply to act and then let go. Only action that is in harmony with the Tao, that is free from desire, can create anything that endures. Remember what the Master does: "When her work is done, she forgets it. That is why it lasts forever" (chapter 2). The idea here is the same. As we've noted before, there is no promise that any of this is easy. But it is simple.

How often we cling to our work. We believe others will judge us by it. We are heavily invested in it. Letting go is the last thing we would do.

Have you ever created something without having your name stamped on it, as it were? Just created something as a gift. Have you ever wondered about "anonymous donors"? Their gift is clearly not about them. We don't even know who they are. For them, their gift is about the difference their gift makes and nothing else. They have let go.

This chapter reminds us that to live in harmony with the Tao, the last thing we need to do is stand on tiptoe, rush ahead, and try to shine a light on ourselves by clinging to our work. It's very much simpler. "Just do your job, then let go."

25

There was something formless and perfect
before the universe was born.
It is serene. Empty.
Solitary. Unchanging.
Infinite. Eternally present.
It is the mother of the universe.
For lack of a better name,
I call it the Tao.

It flows through all things,
inside and outside, and returns
to the origin of all things.

The Tao is great.
The universe is great.
Earth is great.
Man is great.
These are the four great powers.

Man follows the earth.
Earth follows the universe.
The universe follows the Tao.
The Tao follows only itself.

The Tao is eternally present.

Here are some typical questions that the mind comes up with: Where does the Tao come from? Is there anything greater than the Tao? What does the Tao look like?

Well, the short answers are, the Tao does not "come from" anything or anywhere; no, there is nothing greater than it; and the Tao does not "look like" anything, as it has no form. We may recall, the Tao is "form that includes all forms, image without an image, subtle, beyond all conception" (chapter 14). These are not easy words for the mind to grasp.

The longer answer, if you want to think of things "coming from" other things, looks like this: Think of human beings as coming from the earth. Think of the earth as coming from the universe. Think of the universe as coming from the Tao. Then think of the Tao as "the mother of the universe." But note that we haven't defined it by naming it and pinning it down in space and time. In fact we can't really even name it. The best we can do is point to it and be aware that's all we're doing. "For lack of a better name, I call it the Tao."

So our sequence goes human beings, earth, universe, Tao. The Tao, if you like, is at the end of the line. But unlike human beings, the earth, and the universe, it has no form. So it doesn't really "fit" anywhere in space. The Tao was there "before the universe was born." But unlike human beings, the earth, and the universe, it always was and always will be and, therefore, doesn't really "fit" anywhere in time either. If anything, we'd have to say it is "eternally present." Another thought that's not easy to grasp.

All right then, so the Tao is beyond space and time. Is there anything we can say about the Tao? The short answer is, not really. The longer answer is that we could attempt to describe it with words such as "formless," "perfect," "serene," "empty," "solitary," "unchanging," and "infinite." But what do these words tell us? They tell us that the Tao is too big a concept for us to get our minds around. In fact the Tao is too big to be thought of as a concept. In fact it is too big to be thought of as "too big." In fact it is too big to be thought of. In fact it just "is."

If the Tao is anything (which it isn't), then it is everything and every thing. But what do we mean by that? Well, how about this: "It flows through all things, inside and outside, and returns to the origin of all things." It is not only at the end of the line, it is also at the beginning of the line; it is the line. Ideally, our minds would fall quiet on becoming aware of this truth and we would become silent, still, serene, and empty as we become aware that all separation is illusion and unity is reality. But typically our minds chatter on as we try to pin down the Tao into some thought structure.

For example, is the Tao greater than mankind, is it greater than the earth, is it greater than the universe? The answer is, they're all great. "These are the four great powers." If you must impose some order, then "man follows the earth. Earth follows the universe. The universe follows the Tao." But I know what you're going to ask next. You're going to ask, what does the Tao follow? So we're back at the end of the line again. Or should we say the beginning? Ideally, we shouldn't say anything at all, because the Tao just "is." But if you really want the Tao to follow something, then the best we can do is say, "The Tao follows only itself."

Do these answers satisfy the mind? Not really. Do these answers help us become aware that there is more to living than satisfying the mind? Hopefully they do. If so, then we are one step closer to dwelling in harmony with the Tao.

How often we forget about things greater than we can wrap our minds around. And as a result, what a small world we tend to live in.

Have you ever looked up at a clear night sky and seen the stars? Millions of them. Billions. Whole galaxies countless light-years away. Have you ever tried to wrap your mind around the concept of a light-year? The thought is humbling, isn't it?

This chapter reminds us that if we're going to hitch ourselves to any star, it had better be something bigger than we can grasp with our minds. How about something so big we cannot even name it? For lack of a better name, we could call it the Tao.

The heavy is the root of the light.
The unmoved is the source of all movement.

Thus the Master travels all day
without leaving home.
However splendid the views,
she stays serenely in herself.

Why should the lord of the country
flit about like a fool?
If you let yourself be blown to and fro,
you lose touch with your root.
If you let restlessness move you,
you lose touch with who you are.

Stay rooted in the Tao.

This chapter contrasts the restless person who leaves behind her roots in search of "splendid views" on the journey to discover who she is, and the Master, who is already aware of who she is without going anywhere.

How is it that the Master is already aware of who she is? The answer is that when you dwell in harmony with the Tao, there is no need to travel anywhere else, because you're aware you have already arrived. If we think of life being like a journey, then we might think of awareness as being the destination. This implies a gap between where we are and where we want to be, and a journey we have to undertake to close the gap.

But the trouble with this thinking is that it's the thinking that creates the gap. The gap is an illusion. In reality, awareness is not a destination that is "somewhere else." It is right under our feet all the time. In reality there is no gap, there is no separation, only unity. Separation is illusion. Unity is real. And we can arrive at this awareness in an instant, without going anywhere, the moment we realize there is no "there" to go to.

The trouble is that our minds just don't see it that way. They prefer to think. So we define, we distinguish, and we separate. And in doing so we create the very gaps we then seek to close. In other words, we create the apparent need for the journey. But it doesn't have to be this way.

Let's see what the Master does. She is aware of how the mind creates the need for the journey. This awareness is why she "travels all day without leaving home. However splendid the views, she stays serenely within herself." These words describe what it looks like to have "arrived." We've seen that travel implies an origin, a destination, and movement between the two to close the gap. If you like, the Master "moves" from one to the other without going anywhere, because she is aware that the origin and the destination are the same. Hence, "the unmoved is the source of all movement." The "source" is both the origin and the destination at once.

We think the purpose of our travel is to get in touch with who we are, with what this chapter calls our "root." This is a great image for making the points above, because roots don't move. They're in the ground. They don't go anywhere. If you want to be in touch with your root, then every step of your journey only takes you further from where you want to be. Therefore, to travel in search of something that is under your feet all the time is surely to "flit about like a fool." And then to keep on searching is surely to let yourself "be blown to and fro." All you will accomplish is to separate yourself further from your root.

In summary, to dwell in harmony with the Tao is to be in touch with who you are. To be aware of this, there's no need to move from where you are to anywhere else. In fact, you don't need to move at all. Who you are is like a root. It's right under your feet. Move anywhere else and you lose touch with it. If you want splendid views then look inside. The only country is yourself. The only journey to take lies within.

So how does the Master arrive? By staying "serenely within herself." She is in touch with her root. She knows who she is. No movement is required.

How often we believe happiness and fulfillment lie somewhere other than where we are. If we are feeling neither of those things, then surely we have to go somewhere else to find them. And so we undertake the journey.

But have you ever stopped to wonder whether what you're chasing is no more than a desire. Desires come and go like the wind. Chase after them and you will indeed "be blown to and fro." Have you ever satisfied a desire only to find another one pop up to take its place? Chase after the new one and you will indeed "flit about like a fool."

This chapter reminds us that happiness and fulfillment follow from being at home in yourself. They are the fruit, if you like, of being rooted in who you already are. There is no need to go anywhere.

27

A good traveler has no fixed plans
and is not intent upon arriving.
A good artist lets his intuition
lead him wherever it wants.
A good scientist has freed himself of concepts
and keeps his mind open to what is.

Thus the Master is available to all people
and doesn't reject anyone.
He is ready to use all situations
and doesn't waste anything.
This is called embodying the light.

What is a good man but a bad man's teacher?
What is a bad man but a good man's job?
If you don't understand this, you will get lost,
however intelligent you are.
It is the great secret.

Embody the light.

To dwell in harmony with the Tao is to embody the light. We've seen this image before. "The Master keeps her mind always at one with the Tao; this is what gives her her radiance" (chapter 21). "Because he doesn't display himself, people can see his light" (chapter 22).

What does it mean to "embody the light"? It means to meet life without preconceptions as to what life should be or how it should unfold. This is not easy, because much of the time we act with narrow-minded intention. Our minds therefore tend to be closed. We make judgments as we accept some things and reject others based on whether they fit our plans. We are available to some people if it suits our purposes but are unavailable to others. As a result, we waste situations as we miss opportunities that we are too blind and closed-minded to see.

So how do we avoid acting in narrow-minded ways? What follows are three examples of this idea in action: the traveler, the artist, and the scientist. The good traveler "has no fixed plans and is not intent upon arriving." At first glance, we may be tempted to label such a traveler as aimless and purposeless. (How swift we are to judge.) Of course a traveler has an origin and a destination but, if he is aware, he realizes that the purpose lies in the journey, not in the actual arrival.

Similarly, the good artist realizes inspiration does not come from commands issued by his mind. It comes from letting go, keeping his mind silent, and letting his intuition lead him where it will. The good scientist realizes preconceived concepts can get in the way. They tend to clutter the mind, making it full and unable to receive new insights. He recognizes the need to empty the mind to make room for the new, to ensure his mind is open and not closed. "A good scientist has freed himself of concepts and keeps his mind open to what is." (Note the implication that concepts imprison, and that a closed mind fails to see what is. These are strong words.)

In summary, if we're not careful, we tend to have fixed plans, intention focused only on arriving, disregard for intuition, and closed minds. The result is that we miss and waste opportunities. This is not the way to go.

What would the Master do? The exact opposite. He would have no fixed plans, would let himself be guided by his intuition, and would keep his mind open. And look at the result: "The Master is available to all people and doesn't reject anyone. He is ready to use all situations and doesn't waste anything." What is this? "This is called embodying the light." There we have it. No limit. No judgment. Nothing wasted.

A final example brings this point home. We might think a "good man" would be nothing but wasted time to a "bad man." And we might think a bad man has nothing to teach a good man. Again, the opposite is true. When both are open to each other, then each has something to give and to receive. "What is a good man but a bad man's teacher? What is a bad man but a good man's job?" Of course, there can be no teaching without the teacher seeing the opportunity for what it is and being "available." And there can be no learning without the student having an open mind.

In closing, we're reminded that it is not enough merely to be intelligent and grasp these ideas intellectually. What matters is what we do with them, how we embody them in our daily living. "If you don't understand this, you will get lost, however intelligent you are."

But is this truth really a "great secret"? No. If anything, it is blindingly obvious. But, blinded by habit, we simply don't see it. The words and images in this chapter are written to help us see.

How often we try to force fit reality into our idea of what it should be. We accept some things and reject others, including people.

Have you ever let your intuition lead you wherever it wants and kept your mind truly open to what is? And, when you have done this, have you ever found that the situation that unfolded was in fact better than whatever you previously had in mind?

This chapter reminds us that when we are truly open to what is, we are beyond accepting and rejecting. We waste nothing. We have stepped aside. We're not blocking the light. In fact, we're doing the opposite: we're "embodying the light."

28

Know the male,
yet keep to the female:
receive the world in your arms.
If you receive the world,
the Tao will never leave you
and you will be like a little child.

Know the white,
yet keep to the black:
be a pattern for the world.
If you are a pattern for the world,
the Tao will be strong inside you
and there will be nothing you can't do.

Know the personal,
yet keep to the impersonal:
accept the world as it is.
If you accept the world,
the Tao will be luminous inside you
and you will return to your primal self.

The world is formed from the void,
like utensils from a block of wood.
The Master knows the utensils,
yet keeps to the block:
thus she can use all things.

Accept the world.

The Tao contains no commandments, only observations that provide opportunities for insights. What we do with the insights is up to us. But acting on them has predictable consequences. This chapter contains three such observations: "receive the world in your arms," "be a pattern for the world," and "accept the world as it is." Each is presented in terms of cause and effect; and the consequences for each are spelled out. If we do X, then what that means with respect to the Tao is Y. The common theme is to be aware, to act, but to make no judgments. You thereby embrace everything and waste nothing, and the Tao can shine through you. Let's look at each observation.

Male is balanced by female. Neither is better than the other. Both are part of the world. Both are yours to receive. If you receive them, then you will dwell serenely in harmony with the Tao, as safe as a child in its mother's arms. "If you receive the world, the Tao will never leave you and you will be like a little child."

White is balanced by black. Neither is better than the other. Both are part of the world. Act in constant awareness of this and you will be a pattern for the world. If you do this, then you allow the Tao to fill you with strength. "If you are a pattern for the world, the Tao will be strong inside you and there will be nothing you can't do."

The personal is balanced by the impersonal. Neither is better than the other. Both are part of the world. Typically, we see the world in terms of how well it conforms to our desires and judge and reject accordingly instead of simply accepting "the world as it is." To the extent that we are full of our desires, we separate ourselves from the Tao. When our desires and our self-images, or egos, dictate our actions, they bury our true inner selves and we block the light instead of embodying it (as described in the last chapter). On the other hand, "if you accept the world, the Tao will be luminous inside you and you will return to your primal self." It is our primal self that will shine if only we let it. And we succeed by simply not separating ourselves from the Tao in the first place. "The Master keeps her mind always at one with the Tao; this is what gives her her radiance" (chapter 21).

Only when we stand back far enough can we be aware of the Oneness/Wholeness of everything. It is when we look at the world up close, through our mind's eye, that we start to define, to make distinctions, and to name the apparently separate things we think we see. When we then go on to see those things in terms of our desires, we separate ourselves even further from reality. We may recall that "naming is the origin of all particular things. Free from desire, you realize the mystery. Caught in desire, you see only the manifestations" (chapter 1). Caught in desire, we judge things in terms of whether they serve our purposes and accept or reject them accordingly.

On the other hand, when we're in harmony with the Tao, we are aware of the Oneness/Wholeness of all things. We accept everything and reject nothing. We are free from the desire to have the world be anything other than the way it is, and our actions can spring from our "primal self," or our true inner self, as opposed to our self-image, or ego. Nothing is wasted. Everything can be used.

The Master is constantly aware of both the Oneness/Wholeness of everything and the separate "manifestations," but she makes no judgments, accepts all of them, and so can use all of them. "The world is formed from the void, like utensils from a block of wood. The Master knows the utensils, yet keeps to the block: thus she can use all things." As a result she is luminous. She is strong. There is nothing she can't do.

How often we selectively accept and reject bits and pieces of the world according to whether they conform to our desires. We accept what we want and reject what we cannot use. We see whatever we don't want as useless. Strangely enough, this is exactly what limits us.

Do you remember when you were a "little child"? You entrusted yourself to the world around you because you hadn't lived long enough to conceive of a "better" version of the world to strive for. You were able to relax in your parents' arms—accepting everything, rejecting nothing.

This chapter reminds us that we can trust the Tao in exactly the same way. When you stop selectively accepting and rejecting, when you see nothing as useless, when you accept the world as it is, that is when "the Tao will be luminous inside you" and you will discover that "there will be nothing you can't do."

29

Do you want to improve the world?
I don't think it can be done.

The world is sacred.
It can't be improved.
If you tamper with it, you'll ruin it.
If you treat it like an object, you'll lose it.

There is a time for being ahead,
a time for being behind;
a time for being in motion,
a time for being at rest;
a time for being vigorous,
a time for being exhausted;
a time for being safe,
a time for being in danger.

The Master sees things as they are,
without trying to control them.
She lets them go their own way,
and resides at the center of the circle.

See things as they are.

The message of this chapter can be summarized in three words: "let it be." Typically, we don't let it be. Instead we continually seek to change things in the world around us. Why? Because we think we know better. We think the world isn't good enough the way it is and we think we are the ones to improve it. And we want to do it our way.

But let's look at the assumptions behind this thinking. "Not good enough," says who? "It can be improved"; who else agrees? "We know what needs to be done"; do we really? "And we are the ones to do the improving"; why do we think so? There are four assumptions here. If any one of them is not true, then our attempts at "improvements" are, at best, vain tampering and, at worst, destructive. That's quite a downside for getting it wrong. We might say, yes but our intentions are good; after all, we're only trying to improve things. I'm sorry, but that's not much consolation.

The trouble lies in the word "improvement," because it represents a judgment. So let's suspend judgment for a moment and see what happens. What if the world were already perfect, not in need of either your idea of improvement or mine. Then where would we be?

In fact, let's take this one step further, because the word "perfect" invites us to think of "less than perfect," which we might interpret as justification for our self-appointed roles as improvers. So let's take the step. What if the world simply is what it is? Neither good nor bad. Then where would we be? We would simply accept things are as they are without trying to control and improve them. We would let them be. That's exactly what this chapter invites us to consider. "The world is sacred. It can't be improved. If you tamper with it, you'll ruin it. If you treat it like an object, you'll lose it." These words don't leave much to the imagination.

The reality is that things come and they go. We delude ourselves if we think we can control them all. Each comes and goes in its own time, which is not at our command. What follows here is a string of examples: a time for being ahead or behind, in motion or at rest, vigorous or exhausted, safe or in danger. Do we get to decide when each of these times is to be? Not really. Do we get to create stress and anxiety for ourselves by thinking that we do? Certainly; we do it all the time. Does it need to be this way? No, it doesn't.

Let's see what the Master does. "The Master sees things as they are, without trying to control them. She lets them go their own way and resides at the center of the circle." We may recall the observation to "just stay at the center of the circle and let all things take their course" (chapter 19). The idea here is the same. The circle gets us thinking beyond opposites like good and bad or right and wrong. Think of them as arranged along the rim of a circle instead of as polar opposites. Are any of them now any "better" than any others? It's harder to make a judgment now. So don't try. Suspend judgment. Just reside at the center of the circle and let them be.

But does refraining from trying to control things and making judgments about them mean we don't act? Are we just passive blobs watching the world go its own way? Do we drop out? Not at all. Certainly we can act and be fully engaged in this world. The point is that our actions do not need to spring from judgment, or ego, or desire to impose our ideas of "improvements" upon the world. On the contrary, "Giving birth and nourishing, having without possessing, acting with no expectations, leading and not trying to control; this is the supreme virtue" (chapter 10). This is what the Master does. Doing so doesn't sound like dropping out to me.

How often we try to impose our ideas of improvements upon the world. And when we do, we treat the world exactly like an object that can be tampered with. And how often do we succeed? And how long-lasting is our success?

Have you ever seen things as they are without trying to control them? Sometimes you've been ahead, other times you've been behind. Sometimes in motion, sometimes at rest. "It's all good" is a popular catch-phrase we like to use. But what if it were literally true? If it were all good, then nothing would need "improvement." In that case, wouldn't the best thing we could do be to "let it be"?

This chapter reminds us to do exactly this.

30

Whoever relies on the Tao in governing men
doesn't try to force issues
or defeat enemies by force of arms.
For every force there is a counterforce.
Violence, even well intentioned,
always rebounds upon oneself.

The Master does his job
and then stops.
He understands that the universe
is forever out of control,
and that trying to dominate events
goes against the current of the Tao.
Because he believes in himself,
he doesn't try to convince others.
Because he is content with himself,
he doesn't need others' approval.
Because he accepts himself,
the whole world accepts him.

Go with the current of the Tao.

The last chapter talked about our attempts to improve the world. "Do you want to improve the world? I don't think it can be done" (chapter 29). This chapter goes further. Not only can it not be done, but if we try to force issues, then our attempts will backfire on us.

For example, consider the business of governing men. One option is "to force issues or defeat enemies by force of arms." But does this result in long-term harmony? Perhaps one army could defeat another in a single battle, or even go on to win several battles and win a war. But is this where long-term victory lies? We should at least ask ourselves the question. So let's do it. If we step back from the battle, and then further back from the war, what exactly have we achieved?

This chapter says that using force is like pushing against a spring. Energy builds up that will eventually push back. "For every force there is a counterforce. Violence, even well intentioned, always rebounds upon oneself." And when it rebounds, then where are we? Likely back where we started and having incurred much needless pain and suffering along the way. Is this what we wanted? I doubt it. So what exactly have we achieved? Less than nothing?

What does the Master do? He also acts with intention, but there is a critical difference. The difference is that he does not try to impose his intention on others or force issues or dominate events. Instead, "the Master does his job and then stops." He is aware that the Tao is like a current with its own flow. To act in harmony with the Tao is to go with the flow and help the universe unfold, with no expectation as to what the result should look like.

Because he has no expectation, the Master stops when he has done his job. He does not linger, anxiously waiting to see if his actions have the preconceived outcome he desires, poised to interfere, control, and dominate events if they don't turn out exactly as he wanted. "He understands that the universe is forever out of control, and that trying to dominate events goes against the current of the Tao." (Note that the universe is "out of control" only to the mind that seeks to dominate and force its desires upon the world.) Thus the Master acts, stops, and lets go. He acts with intention, not with expectation. Letting go is what makes the difference.

Typically, much of what we do is an attempt to convince others to believe in us, give us their approval, and accept us. We believe that their belief in us and their approval and acceptance exist outside ourselves and that we need to win them in order to have them. So we start the winning process, and if we don't get what we want, then we start forcing issues. More of this and we eventually get battles and wars.

The trouble is that we're looking in the wrong place. The answers lie within. The only person who needs to believe in you is you. So why try to convince others to believe in you? The only person who needs to be content with you is you. So why act in order to obtain the approval of others? The only person who needs to accept you is you. The Master knows this. He believes in himself, is content with himself, and accepts himself. He is aware that belief, contentment, and acceptance come from within and that he already has them. He doesn't need to get others to provide them for him. This leaves him free from desire and therefore available to dwell in harmony with the Tao.

Paradoxically, it is because he doesn't need acceptance from the world that "the whole world accepts him." The Master really doesn't care one way or the other. He is too busy dwelling in the Tao. And what does this look like? Instead of trying to force issues, it consists of acting with compassion, guided by wisdom, and letting go. We'll say more about this soon.

How often we try to dominate events and force issues. And how often we try to convince others or seek their approval. Yet we know the strength we feel when we believe in ourselves and have the courage of our own convictions.

Do you remember the last time you felt this way? You didn't need approval from others. You just did your job and then stopped. This is what the Master does, acting in harmony with the Tao.

This chapter reminds us that to go with the current of the Tao is to accept ourselves. And it so happens that when we no longer need the approval of others, the world will accept us too.

Weapons are the tools of violence;
all decent men detest them.

Weapons are the tools of fear;
a decent man will avoid them
except in the direst necessity
and, if compelled, will use them
only with the utmost restraint.
Peace is his highest value.
If the peace has been shattered,
how can he be content?
His enemies are not demons,
but human beings like himself.
He doesn't wish them personal harm.
Nor does he rejoice in victory.
How could he rejoice in victory
and delight in the slaughter of men?

He enters a battle gravely,
with sorrow and with great compassion,
as if he were attending a funeral.

Defend the Tao.

What happens when push comes to shove? Does the Master look the other way, or does he step into the fray? The answer is that he steps into the fray but with reluctance, sorrow, and compassion.

This chapter follows directly from the last one, which talked about how the Master "doesn't try to force issues or defeat enemies by force of arms." It went on to say that he "understands that the universe is forever out of control, and that trying to dominate events goes against the current of the Tao" (chapter 30). From these words one might conclude that, when threatened with force or violence, the Master would back down, as it were, and let events take their course.

Not so. The Master will act with force but only when all other possibilities have been exhausted. Why? Because like all "decent men" he detests weapons as being the tools of force, violence, and fear. "Peace is his highest value. If the peace has been shattered, how can he be content?"

So why should the Master be reluctant to do whatever it takes to restore peace? Well, for a start, he knows that "for every force there is a counterforce. Violence, even well intentioned, always rebounds upon oneself" (chapter 30). So he knows that if he resorts even to "well intentioned" violence, then peace will remain shattered, at least for the short term. Using violence to combat violence is like thinking two wrongs will make a right. They don't. But nor can a decent man sit back and watch. Hence the Master will avoid force, violence, and weapons, "except in the direst necessity and, if compelled, will use them only with the utmost restraint."

The "direst necessity" is a sad occasion, because when people resort to violence they harm one another. There is nothing impersonal about this. People get hurt. This is why the Master uses violence only with the "utmost restraint." He knows harm will be done but he wants to minimize it. He is aware that "his enemies are not demons, but human beings like himself. He doesn't wish them personal harm."

Furthermore, once we have resorted to violence, then, in a personal sense, we have all lost, because there can be no real victory once harm has been done. There can be nothing to rejoice about. "How could he rejoice in victory and delight in the slaughter of men?" A battle may be won, but at what price? Before the Master enters the battle, harm has already been done. And he is aware that more will be done in spite of his intention to exercise the utmost restraint. The peace has already been shattered, and he is about to shatter it more.

However you look at it, using violence to restore peace is a sad paradox. Phrases like "well-intentioned violence" or "compassionate violence" are contradictions in terms. They make no sense. And they all represent tragic failures. We may read in the news today sentences like "attempts will be made to minimize collateral damage." But, excuse me, that still means innocent bystanders will get hurt, doesn't it? Yes, it does. This isn't a pity. It's tragic. This is why the Master "enters a battle gravely, with sorrow and with great compassion, as if he were attending a funeral." Peace is already dead and buried. There can be no rejoicing.

But the point is that the Master does enter the battle. When push comes to shove, he will push back. He will act with compassion to restore harmony with the Tao.

How often we see peace being shattered. And when we do, how often we step aside, not wanting to become involved. In all fairness, this is a tough call, because it involves distinguishing situations where we should let events take their course without interference, from those where the Tao needs to be defended, as it were.

Have you ever hesitated like this? A good question to ask yourself is whether the action you're about to take is just you imposing your will or truly a selfless attempt to restore the balance of the Tao. If it's the latter, you are on solid ground.

This chapter reminds us that the decision described above is still a tough call. And if we enter the fray, it is a last resort and we do it gravely, with sorrow and compassion. But we do it.

32

The Tao can't be perceived.
Smaller than an electron,
it contains uncountable galaxies.

If powerful men and women
could remain centered in the Tao,
all things would be in harmony.
The world would become a paradise.
All people would be at peace,
and the law would be written in their hearts.

When you have names and forms,
know that they are provisional.
When you have institutions,
know where their functions should end.
Knowing when to stop,
you can avoid any danger.

All things end in the Tao
as rivers flow into the sea.

Remain centered in the Tao.

Can we wrap our minds around the Tao? No, we can't. Is the Tao big or small? The answer is yes and no. It doesn't matter which. You pick. Of course, this leaves us none the wiser. "Smaller than an electron, it contains uncountable galaxies." It's impossible to wrap your mind around that, isn't it? We're reminded of the lines "Look, and it can't be seen. Listen, and it can't be heard. Reach, and it can't be grasped" (chapter 14).

The point is not to try to perceive the Tao or try to pin it down with definition, but simply to live in harmony with it. "If powerful men and women could remain centered in the Tao, all things would be in harmony. The world would become a paradise." The Tao is not about rules and laws and institutions. If everyone lived in harmony with the Tao, then nothing would need to be spelled out and written down. "All people would be at peace, and the law would be written in their hearts."

We may recall the following lines: "Throw away holiness and wisdom, and the people will be a hundred times happier. Throw away morality and justice, and people will do the right thing. Throw away industry and profit, and there won't be any thieves" (chapter 19). The idea here is the same. It's not the concepts that matter; it's living them out in our daily lives. That's what it's all about.

However, we are human beings, and not all of us naturally live in harmony with the Tao all the time. So that's why we need to spell things out and write them down. We call this making laws. And then we need to have organizations that maintain the laws. We call them institutions. But the point is that they are no more than a means to an end. They are not ends in themselves.

It would be great if we didn't need them at all. So let's look forward to the day when we won't need them anymore and, in the meantime, think of them as merely provisional. "When you have names and forms, know that they are provisional." In the meantime, unfortunately, we do need them. They're like a necessary evil. So let's be sure to draw the lines clearly around where they should begin and end. "When you have institutions, know where their functions should end. Knowing when to stop, you can avoid any danger."

What is this danger? The danger is that, when we don't draw lines, it is easy for laws and institutions to run away with us and become ends in themselves. When this happens we lose sight of their purpose. This is not good. The purpose is not to conform to the law for the sake of conforming to the law. The purpose of laws should be to help us live in harmony with the Tao. We need to never forget this. For example, we don't refrain from speeding past a school merely because it's against the law. We don't speed because speeding is dangerous and children may get hurt. And, just in case we should temporarily forget, the law is there to remind us.

Looking around in today's world, it's not hard to find examples of laws that have become so complicated that it is as if they have run away with themselves. Nor is it hard to find examples of institutions so filled with their self-importance that it is as if they have forgotten why they were formed. But if we could get it right, then "the world would become a paradise." Just imagine what that would be like. John Lennon wrote a song about this same beautiful idea.

In the end, it's all about living in harmony with the Tao. "All things end in the Tao as rivers flow into the sea." Let's see if we can keep it all simple instead of needlessly complex.

How often we complicate our world with rules and regulations. And then we need institutions to maintain and enforce them. And thus we build our bureaucratic organizations that so often seem to interfere with our lives.

Have you ever wondered how compliance with rules and regulations seems to be what matters? Compliance is a practical matter. After all, you break the law or you don't. But how seldom we step back and ask ourselves: What is the underlying principle at stake in this situation?

This chapter reminds us to step back and not forget the big picture. In the end, what is it all about? And the answer is, it's about living in harmony with the Tao. If we truly focused on doing so, the need for rules and regulations would disappear and "the world would become a paradise." How do we do this? Remain centered in the Tao.

33

Knowing others is intelligence;
knowing yourself is true wisdom.
Mastering others is strength;
mastering yourself is true power.

If you realize that you have enough,
you are truly rich.
If you stay in the center
and embrace death with your whole heart,
you will endure forever.

Master your self.

What is the difference between intelligence and true wisdom? The first applies to how well you know others and the second to how well you know yourself. What's the difference between strength and true power? The first is about mastering others and the second about mastering yourself. The idea is the same in both comparisons. You can be as intelligent and strong as you like in knowing and mastering others, but it is in self-knowledge and self-mastery that "true wisdom" and "true power" lie.

Typically, we look outside ourselves in our search for happiness and control of our world. We tend to think that if we can get others to do what we want, then we will be happy. But there are two problems with this. First, we can never really succeed in controlling others. Second, even if we could, there's no guarantee we would be happy as a result. Why? Because happiness, or peace and serenity, is not the product of something we do to anything or anybody in the outside world. It is the result of knowing and mastering our self.

Similarly, we can be easily distracted by the pursuit of riches in the outside world. However, we may recall the words "Chase after money and security and your heart will never unclench" (chapter 9). This saying is true because typically we don't know when to stop chasing. However much we have, we are constantly tempted to think that more will be better. Indeed our society has developed a whole marketing and advertising industry dedicated to keeping us in a constant state of never having "enough" and constantly wanting more.

But if you buy into this thinking (pun intended), you'll find yourself caught up in the endless pursuit of money and security and will spend your life worrying about the future instead of living in the present moment. Your heart will never "unclench" and you will never know happiness, peace, and serenity. There is only one way to unclench, and that is to stop chasing.

So when should you stop? Maybe you'll stop chasing money when you're truly rich. But what exactly is "truly rich"? How will you know when you have arrived? Well, the answer is, you have already arrived and the time to stop is right now. Most likely you already have more than enough. "If you realize that you have enough, you are truly rich." The instant you are aware of this, the need to chase after more disappears. You have stopped. Finally.

Remember the image of the circle? "The Master sees things as they are . . . and resides at the center of the circle" (chapter 29). The same image is here with the same message. What matters is not what's at the edge of the circle—knowing others, mastering others, and forever chasing more riches on the outside. What matters is what's at the center. You. Knowing and mastering yourself. Realizing you already have enough and that you are already truly rich.

So stop worrying about life and whether you have enough money, security, and possessions. Here's a question that may help: ask yourself, when you die, will you take any of them with you? Of course not. None of them last. None of them are enduring. So, for a moment, imagine you're already dead. Do you need all those riches now? No, you don't. So embrace death and you become free to truly live.

"If you stay at the center and embrace death with your whole heart, you will endure forever."

How often we are distracted by riches and possessions. A faster car, a bigger house. A second car, a second house. Really? Is this where peace and serenity lie?

Have you ever put on the brakes for a moment and asked yourself where you're headed and when you think you will arrive? Most of the time the honest answer would be that you're not sure and you don't know. But the trouble is, we tend to carry on regardless.

This chapter reminds us that when we continue chasing money, possessions, and security regardless of already having enough, we're looking outward and living on the edge. The place to look is inward. The place to dwell is the center. It's not the outside world we need to master, with its riches and possessions. What we need to master is ourselves.

34

The great Tao flows everywhere.
All things are born from it,
yet it doesn't create them.
It pours itself into its work,
yet it makes no claim.
It nourishes infinite worlds,
yet it doesn't hold on to them.
Since it is merged with all things
and hidden in their hearts,
it can be called humble.
Since all things vanish into it
and it alone endures,
it can be called great.
It isn't aware of its greatness;
thus it is truly great.

The Tao is merged with all things.

"The great Tao flows everywhere. All things are born from it." Two of the most common images for the Tao are of flowing everywhere and of being what everything is born from. Here are a couple more examples: "All things end in the Tao as rivers flow into the sea" (chapter 32). "Infinite. Eternally present. It is the mother of the universe" (chapter 25).

In the big picture, the Tao is everything and every thing is part of the Tao. But the trouble with the big picture is that it's difficult to grasp and identify with, not least of all because, at the level of Oneness/Wholeness, our identity disappears. So let's work with a smaller picture, one in which we can see ourselves. This chapter personifies the Tao to help us do exactly that. It does this by talking about the Tao as if it had "work" to do. The point of this is to help us approach our work in the same way the Tao does and thus live in harmony with it.

So here goes. If the Tao had work to do (which of course it doesn't, because it simply "is"), then it would "pour itself into its work." It would bring forth life in the same way that a mother gives birth while being aware that she is not creating what is born. The Tao does this, except on an unimaginably large scale. "The Tao is called the Great Mother: empty yet inexhaustible, it gives birth to infinite worlds" (chapter 6).

But here's the critical difference between the "work" of the Tao and what we typically do. We typically identify ourselves with our work. We see ourselves as the creators. We claim our work as our own. We hold on to it. We don't let go. We desire others to notice what we think we have accomplished and associate it with us. We work to gain the esteem of others. We want them to see us as "great." We have great expectations.

In contrast, look at how the Tao does its work. "It doesn't create." "It makes no claim." "It doesn't hold on." We may recall, "The Master doesn't seek fulfillment. Not seeking, not expecting, she is present, and can welcome all things" (chapter 15). To live in harmony with the Tao is to see yourself as a part of all things, as merged with all things, as having no identity with which greatness can be associated. Since the Tao "is merged with all things and hidden in their hearts, it can be called humble." This is the spirit in which we should approach our work.

"Giving birth and nourishing, having without possessing, acting with no expectations, leading and not trying to control: this is the supreme virtue" (chapter 10).

It's only when we let go of expectation that our work endures. It's only when we realize that being great in the eyes of others is not the point that, paradoxically, we become "great"—at the precise moment when it no longer matters to us. We've seen this before. "When you are content to be simply yourself and don't compare or compete, everybody will respect you" (chapter 8). Only when we stop focusing on ourselves and comparing ourselves with others do we become free to live in harmony with the Tao.

"If you want to accord with the Tao, just do your job, then let go" (chapter 24). "Because she has let go of herself, she is perfectly fulfilled" (chapter 7). Thus perfect fulfillment lies in doing your work and letting go of all expectation. The Tao "isn't aware of its greatness; thus it is truly great." "It alone endures." The message is clear.

How often we seek greatness. We claim our creations and hold on to them. We're not interested in being "merged with all things." Vanishing is the last thing on our mind. After all, how can someone invisible be seen as great?

There's a saying in the business world, that there's no limit to what you can accomplish when you don't mind who takes the credit. What if we let this principle guide all our actions?

This chapter reminds us that the moment we don't mind who takes the credit is the moment we let go instead of holding on. When we do this, we have got beyond the flash in the pan of greatness. What we create will now endure. Just like the Tao.

35

She who is centered in the Tao
can go where she wishes, without danger.
She perceives the universal harmony,
even amid great pain,
because she has found peace in her heart.

Music or the smell of good cooking
may make people stop and enjoy.
But words that point to the Tao
seem monotonous and without flavor.
When you look for it, there is nothing to see.
When you listen for it, there is nothing to hear.
When you use it, it is inexhaustible.

The Tao is inexhaustible.

The last chapter invited us to consider how the Tao, as it were, "pours itself into its work," "doesn't create," "makes no claim," and "doesn't hold on." The first few lines of this chapter describe what happens when we adopt the same approach. When we live "centered in the Tao," we find three things: freedom, harmony, and inner peace. Let's look at each in turn.

Freedom is described as being able to go where you wish "without danger." What is the danger? The danger lies in "making claims" and "holding on." It lies in living in response to our typical desire to fulfill our expectations. The most dangerous of these is the desire is to be thought well of by others, to inflate our self-esteem or boost our ego, and then to use our actions as a means to this end.

Harmony is described as being perceived "even amid great pain." What is the pain? Typically we experience pain as immediate, even if we see others experiencing it. But if we stand back far enough to see the big picture, then pain is simply part of what is. In this respect, it is no better or worse than pleasure or happiness. Both are equally part of the great Oneness/Wholeness. So what does this mean? Does it mean we don't do anything about pain? No, we still act with compassion. But our first step is acceptance. First, we see pain in the context of the big picture. Then we get to work on our part of the smaller, immediate picture, where we can act with compassion to make a difference.

Third, inner peace is described as being the cause of freedom and harmony: ". . . because she has found peace in her heart." And the cause of inner peace is, of course, being centered in the Tao. So the sequence goes like this: Being centered in the Tao causes inner peace. Inner peace causes us to perceive universal harmony. Awareness of universal harmony causes us to be able to go freely where we wish without danger of getting tangled up in desire and expectation. However, these words suggest a chain reaction of cause and effect. The reality is that they all happen at once.

The trouble with words is that they can never describe the Tao. The best they can do is point to it. The words themselves are not the point (pun intended). Words are "monotonous and without flavor." They are not real and down-to-earth, like music or the smell of good cooking. A couple of good down-to-earth images! Music is, of course, anything but monotonous, and good cooking is anything but without flavor. "The smell of good cooking may make people stop and enjoy." It is the stopping and enjoying that is real. This is what matters.

What this means is that to live in harmony, to stop and enjoy life, we need to look past the words. The Tao simply cannot be described. "When you look for it, there is nothing to see. When you listen for it, there is nothing to hear." We have come across this before. "Look, and it can't be seen. Listen, and it can't be heard. Reach, and it can't be grasped" (chapter 14).

Yet when we are centered in the Tao and living in harmony with it, there is nothing we cannot do. "When you use it, it is inexhaustible." This is the amazing part. "The Tao is . . . empty yet inexhaustible. . . . It is always present within you. You can use it any way you want" (chapter 6). The more you think about it, the more incredible this is—until you realize that thinking about it is not the point. The point is to live it in our daily lives.

How often we live our lives up close and personal. We do not step back anywhere near far enough to see the universal harmony. We are not centered in the Tao, and chances are we do not have peace in our heart.

A good example of something up close and personal is the sound of music or the smell of good cooking. We enjoy them both and there is nothing wrong with either of them. And we have all sorts of words for describing them.

But this chapter reminds us that when we are centered in the Tao, we step back far beyond what words can describe. When we look for the Tao we don't find anything we can name. When we listen for it we don't find anything we can hear. But when we are centered in it and use it, what we do find is that it is inexhaustible.

36

If you want to shrink something,
you must first allow it to expand.
If you want to get rid of something,
you must first allow it to flourish.
If you want to take something,
you must first allow it to be given.
This is called the subtle perception
of the way things are.

The soft overcomes the hard.
The slow overcomes the fast.
Let your workings remain a mystery.
Just show people the results.

How to work with the Tao.

How do you bring about change? More specifically, changes to things in our outside world. We may recall, chapter 22 talked about changing things within ourselves. "If you want to become whole, let yourself be partial. If you want to become straight, let yourself be crooked. If you want to become full, let yourself be empty. If you want to be reborn, let yourself die." The key word in all of these is "let." This chapter talks about changing things outside ourselves, and the key word is "allow."

Typically, we believe that when we want something in the outside world to be a certain way, we simply need to make it so. If it doesn't happen easily, then we try harder. If it still doesn't happen, then we force it. But this is not the way to go if we are to live in harmony with the Tao.

Instead, this chapter tells us that we must first allow the opposite of whatever we desire. For example, "If you want to shrink something, you must first allow it to expand." Or "If you want to get rid of something, you must first allow it to flourish." Or "If you want to take something, you must first allow it to be given." What's going on here? Why must we "first allow it" to be anything? Why can't we just make it what we want?

The answer is that the first step in dwelling in the Tao is always awareness and acceptance of the way things are. The second step is to act in harmony with it. Too often we skip the first step. And too often our second step includes no patience for harmony with anything other than our desires. Note that this chapter doesn't say we cannot make changes. It simply tells us to first slow down and be aware of the way things are and accept them as such.

Why? Because if we don't slow down, then we'll see things only in terms of what we want them to be and remain unaware of the way they are. It's like acting with our eyes closed, imagining that what we want things to be is all that matters. But it's not. Here's why. Action driven by desire for change that is not rooted in the Tao will sooner or later result in difficulty and conflict. This is why we need to first perceive things as they are. Only then we can act to make changes. This is why this approach is called "subtle perception."

Why is approaching things this way important? Quite simply, because if you act from this perception, then you will act in harmony with the Tao and you will succeed. So here's the difference between subtle perception and our usual approach. Typically, our approach is to act quickly to "shrink something" or "get rid of something" or "take something." Instead, when we act in awareness of the way things are, our approach becomes different. We find that "the soft overcomes the hard. The slow overcomes the fast." We align ourselves with the Tao instead of simply trying to force our desires on it.

The difference lies in acting from this "subtle perception." It is indeed subtle. You could even call it a mystery. But the labels are not what matters. What matters is what you do and the results you produce. So don't try to explain the mystery. Don't try to describe it, analyze it, and talk about it. Just be aware, act with compassion in harmony with the Tao, let go of desire and expectation, and the results will speak for themselves. "Let your workings remain a mystery. Just show people the results."

How often our perception of the way things are is anything but subtle. Do things meet our expectations and satisfy our desires? If not, then we need to change them, preferably now. There's nothing subtle about that.

But have you ever first paused before acting and become aware of the way things are in terms other than your desires? Things are changing all the time, regardless of what you do. They are expanding, flourishing, and unfolding all on their own. What if you were to align yourself with this flow instead of interfering with it?

This chapter reminds us that our first step should always be to perceive the way things are. Sometimes we may align ourselves with what is naturally unfolding; other times we will still act to make changes. But in either case, our workings will be aligned with the Tao. It is indeed a "subtle perception."

37

The Tao never does anything,
yet through it all things are done.

If powerful men and women
could center themselves in it,
the whole world would be transformed
by itself, in its natural rhythms.
People would be content
with their simple, everyday lives,
in harmony, and free of desire.

When there is no desire,
all things are at peace.

When there is no desire, all things are at peace.

Human beings are always busy doing things. Typically, we have desires and we act to fulfill them. Are we content? Most likely we're content to the extent we succeed in fulfilling our desires. If we're not there yet, then we're not content yet, so we do more things. Surely if we do just a few more things, then our desires will finally be fulfilled and we will know lasting peace, serenity, and contentment? Isn't this the way it goes?

Well, it's certainly one way to go. And if we're not aware, then it's likely the way we're going. This is what we get if we run our lives on automatic pilot and accept the default value of our society, which is always to want more. But will it bring us lasting peace, serenity, and contentment? Not a chance.

Why not? Because there is no end to desire. When will you ever have enough? However much stuff you have, there is always more you can want. Whatever desires you have most recently satisfied can always be replaced by new desires for you to chase after. We may recall, "Chase after money and security and your heart will never unclench" (chapter 9). Keep chasing and you will never know contentment. Chasing stops only when you stop.

Chasing desires is like living on the outer edge of a circle. There is always something further out there to be reached for, somewhere else to try to get to. But there is one place where this is not true, and that is at the center of the circle. At the center, you become aware not only that right here and right now is all there is, but also that you've arrived. You realize there is no "there" to get to. This is it.

What's more, you've already got all you need. When "you realize that you have enough, you are truly rich" (chapter 33). There's no need to "desire" anything. There's no need to chase anything. To be aware of this is to live fully in the present moment. No part of you is desiring something in the future. No part of you is regretting something from the past. Instead, all of you is simply being right here, right now, exactly as you are. This is where peace and serenity lie.

Imagine what would happen if we could do this, or if those who influence others could do this. "If powerful men and women could center themselves in it, the whole world would be transformed by itself, in its natural rhythms." The natural rhythm of the world is to be at the center of the circle and in harmony with the Tao. And what would the result be? "People would be content with their simple, everyday lives, in harmony, and free of desire."

It is desire that disturbs the world's natural rhythm. Desire is what pushes us to the outer edge of the circle in an endless search for something that's under our feet all along. Desire is what makes us want more than our "simple, everyday lives." This is how the chasing starts and how we lose our natural spot at the center. It is simple. "When there is no desire, all things are at peace."

So here's the question: Who decides whether you chase your desires? Who decides whether you run your life on automatic pilot and accept the default value of our society, which is always to want more? Who decides whether you leave the center of the circle? For your answer, all you have to do is look in the mirror. The question now is, what are you going to do about it?

How often we are motivated only by desire. We may even think desire is the only motivating force there is. After all, if we did not desire to achieve our goals, what would motivate us to do anything?

Have you ever wondered what would happen if your goal was simply to live in harmony with the world around you? That doesn't mean you don't do anything. "The Tao never does anything, yet through it all things are done." If you center yourself in the Tao, then what you do becomes part of the harmony. You become part of the natural rhythm. It is through you that things are done.

This chapter reminds us that when we center ourselves in the Tao, we become content. We find that our simple, everyday lives are enough. Peace comes from being in harmony. So what is missing? Desire.

38

The Master doesn't try to be powerful;
thus he is truly powerful.
The ordinary man keeps reaching for power;
thus he never has enough.

The Master does nothing,
yet he leaves nothing undone.
The ordinary man is always doing things,
yet many more are left to be done.

The kind man does something,
yet something remains undone.
The just man does something,
and leaves many things to be done.
The moral man does something,
and when no one responds
he rolls up his sleeves and uses force.

When the Tao is lost, there is goodness.
When goodness is lost, there is morality.
When morality is lost, there is ritual.
Ritual is the husk of true faith,
the beginning of chaos.

Therefore the Master concerns himself
with the depths and not the surface,
with the fruit and not the flower.
He has no will of his own.
He dwells in reality,
and lets all illusions go.

Let all illusions go.

To dwell in harmony with the Tao is to act and then let go. It's the opposite of doing things with desire to fulfill expectations. Follow the path of desire and you will never be done, because there will always be more to try for, more to reach for, more to desire. Thus whatever you try for or reach for will always remain beyond your grasp. Peace lies in freedom from desire. "When there is no desire, all things are at peace" (chapter 37).

For example, reach for power and you will never have enough. On the other hand, stop trying to be powerful and power will come to you. "The Master doesn't try to be powerful; thus he is truly powerful. The ordinary man keeps reaching for power; thus he never has enough."

So what does the Master do? The answer is, he "does" nothing. He simply acts with no expectation of a particular desired outcome. He isn't trying to be anything or to reach for anything. He simply acts with compassion, in harmony with the Tao, and lets go. The result is that his action is complete. "The Master does nothing, yet he leaves nothing undone." In contrast, "the ordinary man is always doing things, yet many more are left to be done." The ordinary man will never finish doing things.

What follows is a series of examples showing this idea in action. Being kind is not enough. Being just is not enough. Being moral and indignant when others fail to respond, and doing what you think is right, is not enough. Why? Because none of these approaches is in harmony with the Tao. In fact they are the result of forgetting the Tao.

We may remember that "when the great Tao is forgotten, goodness and piety appear" (chapter 18). Here we are reminded of this again: "When the Tao is lost, there is goodness." Forget goodness and we fall back on morality. Forget morality and we fall back on ritual. Now we have just about lost it all. "Ritual is the husk of true faith, the beginning of chaos." Strong words.

Living in harmony with the Tao is not about trying to be kind, or trying to be just, or trying to be moral. It's not about "trying to" be anything. These approaches are all superficial. "Therefore the Master concerns himself with the depths and not the surface." The superficial is like a flower, bright and colorful for all to see. But what matters is the result of our actions. This is the fruit. "Therefore the Master concerns himself... with the fruit and not the flower."

The Master has no interest in attracting attention to himself. He is not trying to be kind, or just, or moral, or worthy of any other label that others may confer on him. He knows that if you "care about people's approval... you will be their prisoner" (chapter 9). He knows these labels represent nothing more than the self seeking to inflate its self-image in the eyes of others. The labels are all illusions—the result of the self exercising a will of its own, as it were. In contrast, the Master "has no will of his own. He dwells in reality, and lets all illusions go."

Dwelling in harmony with the Tao is not about doing things or trying to be things. It's about acting and letting go. "Therefore the Master acts without doing anything and teaches without saying anything" (chapter 2). "Doing" is a great distraction. If anything, we should try the opposite. We may recall, "Practice not-doing, and everything will fall into place" (chapter 3). But best of all would be to not try at all. Just do it. As Yoda says, "Try not. Do, or do not. There is no try."

How often we do things trying for a particular result. And when we don't achieve it, what do we do? We try harder.

Have you ever wondered whether trying is part of the problem? What if the other part of the problem lies in thinking there is a particular result we should be trying for in the first place? Perhaps we're not understanding something. Perhaps, in terms of living in harmony with the Tao, we just don't get it.

This chapter reminds us that particular results are always superficial. As such, they are nothing more than illusions. Of course there's a result from what we do, but the question is, where does the action spring from? If it springs from the shallowness of our fleeting desires, then we will reach and reach but there will always be more left to be done. When we do this, we are dwelling in illusion.

It is when our actions spring from the depths that we let go of the desire for particular results. It is when we are centered in the Tao that we dwell in reality. When we act and let go, we are done. This is where peace and serenity lie. Thus the Master "dwells in reality, and lets all illusions go." He gets it.

39

In harmony with the Tao,
the sky is clear and spacious,
the earth is solid and full,
all creatures flourish together,
content with the way they are,
endlessly repeating themselves,
endlessly renewed.

When man interferes with the Tao,
the sky becomes filthy,
the earth becomes depleted,
the equilibrium crumbles,
creatures become extinct.

The Master views the parts with compassion,
because he understands the whole.
His constant practice is humility.
He doesn't glitter like a jewel
but lets himself be shaped by the Tao,
as rugged and common as a stone.

Understand the whole.

Chapter 37 talked about the "natural rhythm" of the world. This chapter describes what this natural rhythm looks like. "In harmony with the Tao, the sky is clear and spacious, the earth is solid and full, all creatures flourish together." This sounds like paradise. Notice an important feature: freedom from desire for things to be anything other than the way they are. "All creatures would flourish together, content with the way things are."

You may remember that if we were centered in the Tao, then "people would be content with their simple everyday lives, in harmony, and free of desire" (chapter 37). The idea here is the same. Desire is what upsets the balance. Natural rhythm is equilibrium. The natural cycle of life is to unfold without interference: "All creatures flourish . . . endlessly repeating themselves, endlessly renewed."

What then follows is a stark contrast showing what happens when people act on their desires, interfere, and upset the balance. "When man interferes with the Tao, the sky becomes filthy, the earth becomes depleted, the equilibrium crumbles, creatures become extinct." This description doesn't leave much to the imagination, does it?

These words capture it all. The pollution caused by our smoke-belching industries, the wastelands caused by merciless strip-mining for minerals or logging for wood, the upset to the balance of nature, and the extinction of species. Can you think of a better description of what happens when we unleash the force of blind commerce, with its endless pursuit of money? This thinking is from 2,500 years ago and it remains just as true today.

The Tao is Oneness/Wholeness in a perfect harmony of endless cycles of renewal. This is the only context for understanding. All the rest are separate parts. None of them is the Whole. It is only when we view the parts in this context that we can act with compassion. The trouble starts when we focus on the parts and forget the Tao. Thus "the Master acts with compassion, because he understands the whole." To constantly interfere with the natural rhythm and upset the balance is to act with arrogance and pride as we pursue our desires for fame and fortune. Look at the Master. "His constant practice is humility."

We saw in the last chapter that "the Master concerns himself with the depths and not the surface, with the fruit and not the flower" (chapter 38). He has no interest in attracting attention to himself or in seeking to inflate his self-image in the eyes of others. "He doesn't glitter like a jewel." He doesn't reach for things or try to possess things. He has no desire for fame and fortune.

So what does he do? He lives in harmony with the Tao, not "seeking" to be anything. "Fluid as melting ice. Shapable as a block of wood. Receptive as a valley. Clear as a glass of water" (chapter 15). The Master doesn't seek to stand out from the crowd. Instead he "lets himself be shaped by the Tao, as rugged and common as a stone." He knows that standing out from the crowd really doesn't matter. All that matters is harmony. The rest is detail.

How often we seek to stand out from the crowd, to glitter like a jewel. We are typically not content with the way things are; such discontent is the root of all desire. It's fine for all creatures to flourish together as long as we get our way. And so we start to interfere to satisfy our desires, and that's when the equilibrium starts to crumble.

Have you ever thought of the world in terms of endless cycles of renewal? We may be tempted to think such cycles would be somehow pointless. After all, what is the point of anything "endlessly repeating" itself? But what if that just happens to be the way things are. What if the point is nothing other than harmony?

This chapter reminds us that only when we understand the world as a whole will we view the parts with compassion. When we act with compassion, we will then not be forcing our desires on the world. We will no longer think the Tao is ours to shape; instead we will allow ourselves be shaped by it. We will become part of the cycle, part of the harmony.

40

Return is the movement of the Tao.
Yielding is the way of the Tao.

All things are born of being.
Being is born of non-being.

Return to the center.

This chapter is particularly succinct. There are doubtless several ways to interpret it.

It reminds me of the image of the circle and how peace and harmony are to be found only at the center. Chasing desires is what keeps us at the edge, focused on what we want as opposed to being "content with the way things are" (chapter 39). "If you realize that you have enough, you are truly rich. If you stay in the center . . . you will endure forever" (chapter 33). "If powerful men and women could center themselves . . . the whole world would be transformed" (chapter 37). So when this chapter says, "Return is the movement of the Tao," I think it's talking about returning to the center.

So how do we return to the center? Here's the good news: Since the Tao is the natural rhythm of the world, all we have to do is allow ourselves to be carried by it. No effort is required. "All things end in the Tao as rivers flow into the sea" (chapter 32). It is only our desires that would have us try to swim upstream. Thus "yielding is the way of the Tao."

But the bad news is, we typically approach this idea with our minds. Here's how it goes: We see returning to the center as something to be "desired." We then make doing so a goal. We then make a plan with milestones and expectations and tasks that consist of doing things to get us to the goal. We may even really get into it and attach future deadlines to the milestones, thus emphasizing that we're not there yet. Then we start striving to do the things necessary to achieve our goal.

Hopefully, however, we may also remember this is not the way to go. Returning to the center calls for none of the machinery of thought. Key words for living in harmony with the Tao are "let" and "allow," as opposed to the push and shove that typically accompany forcing our desires on the world as we execute our preconceived plans. In reality, returning to the center does not call for any effort on our part other than to silence thought and to extinguish desire.

What's going on in the next couple of lines? "All things are born of being. Being is born of non-being." I think this simply reminds us of the great cycle of being. We may remember, "Being and non-being create each other" (chapter 2). "In harmony with the Tao . . . all creatures flourish together . . . endlessly repeating themselves, endlessly renewed" (chapter 39). This is the universe unfolding in harmony and without interference.

So what's our part in all this? It is simply to surrender to the unfolding of the universe, return to the center, and yield to the harmony. Does this mean we turn into passive blobs and do nothing? No, of course not. We are very much alive in the here and now, and this is certainly where we belong for the time being. But harmony results from not being distracted by our self and who we think we are. "We work with being, but non-being is what we use" (chapter 11). Be "content to be simply yourself and don't compare or compete" (chapter 8).

As we have seen elsewhere, living in harmony means understanding the difference between doing things with the expectation of fulfilling our desires and acting with compassion, guided by wisdom, and letting go. When you focus on acting instead of doing, you return to the center and live in harmony with the Tao, aware that "it is always present within you. You can use it any way you want" (chapter 6).

How often what we do takes us further away from the center. We do the opposite of returning. We desire some future state of things, which we see as "out there" and to be strived for. And then we get busy doing the things we think we need to do to achieve this future state.

Have you ever wondered why some of our best memories are from vacations—especially when we were children? On vacation we allow ourselves to step back from the hustle and bustle of our everyday lives. For a period of time, at least, we allow ourselves to be carried by the flow from day to day. We respond to things as they arise and let them go. After all, we have no preconceived desire in mind other than to be on vacation. What if we could take this mindset back to our everyday lives?

This chapter reminds us to return to the center and yield to the Tao. And preferably take a permanent vacation from desire.

41

When a superior man hears of the Tao,
he immediately begins to embody it.
When an average man hears of the Tao,
he half believes it, half doubts it.
When a foolish mans hears of the Tao,
he laughs out loud.
If he didn't laugh,
it wouldn't be the Tao.

Thus it is said:
The path into the light seems dark,
the path forwards seems to go back,
the direct path seems long,
true power seems weak,
true purity seems tarnished,
true steadfastness seems changeable,
true clarity seems obscure,
the greatest art seems unsophisticated,
the greatest love seems indifferent,
the greatest wisdom seems childish.

The Tao is nowhere to be found.
Yet it nourishes and completes all things.

The Tao is everywhere.

What do you do when you hear of the Tao? Well, it all depends on what type of person you are. This chapter contrasts three types of people: a superior one, an average one, and a foolish one. Needless to say, this is done for explanatory purposes only, because there is no meaning in labels like "superior," "average," and "foolish" at the level of the Tao. People simply are as they are. But our minds like to work with distinctions so they can grasp ideas.

So either you immediately begin to embody the Tao, or you half believe it and half doubt it, or you laugh out loud. What's going on here?

We may remember that the only way to embody the Tao is to become still, quiet, and empty. Empty, that is, of all thoughts, particularly ones about yourself, such as who you are and what you desire. This is what's being referred to by the three people described. You're familiar with the phrase "Get over yourself"? Well, if we take that literally, the superior person has completely got over himself, the average person has half got over himself, and the foolish one is still full of himself. This is what determines their responses to the Tao.

If you're empty of your self, there is nothing in the way of the Tao and you can embody it immediately. We may recall, "If you open yourself to the Tao, you are at one with the Tao and you can embody it completely" (chapter 23). To the degree that you're still half-full of your self, you cannot embody the Tao. This is why you half believe it, half doubt it. Finally, if you are still completely full of your self, then there is no room for the Tao at all. You still see your self as separate and not part of it. You don't even see the connection. So how can it possibly be relevant to you? What a joke! You laugh out loud. What else can you do? "If he didn't laugh, it wouldn't be the Tao."

What follows is a long list of things that are not what they seem. And they are all true to the degree that we are still full of our self. Why? Because being full of our self affects everything we see. If our self is still alive and well (and full of itself), then we are not "seeing" things as they are. We are seeing them through the eyes of thought, with all the labels we are so quick to apply to everything "out there." In reality there is no "out there." We are part of "there" and it is a part of us. There is no separation. Separation is illusion. Unity is real. But as long as we still see our self as separate and distinct, then the labels apply to what we think we see.

The first three items in the list refer to the "path" to the Tao. Thus the direct path forward to the light seems to be long, to loop back on itself, and to be dark. When we look at the Master we may think we see him as weak, tarnished, changeable, obscure, unsophisticated, indifferent, and childish—perhaps even an idiot, to use the Master's own words ("I am like an idiot, my mind is so empty," chapter 20). In reality, of course, the Master is the opposite of all these things, if only we could see it. He embodies true power, true purity, true clarity, and true steadfastness. He is full of love, not indifference, and full of wisdom, not childishness. It is because he is empty of himself that he can be full of the Tao, at one with it, dwelling in harmony with it.

In short, the Tao is not out there. We cannot "find" it and bottle it and label it. Why? Because we are not separate from it; we are it, and so is everything else. Thus "the Tao is nowhere to be found. Yet it nourishes and completes all things."

How often we trust appearances. We think things are the way we see them. It doesn't occur to us that we may not see them as they really are. And I think the reason is simple. If it did occur to us, then we'd have to doubt our thoughts. And that's a very uncomfortable thought.

Are you familiar with the phrase, to "suspend judgment"? I'm sure you've done it from time to time. Maybe you've done it a lot. But have you ever wondered what it would be like if you did it all the time? To live with no judging, no labeling. Just living in harmony with what is.

This chapter reminds us that the Tao is everywhere. It is far beyond our ability to grasp it and label it. But, we may think, if it is "nowhere to be found," then can we trust it? Absolutely. After all, it "nourishes and completes all things."

42

The Tao gives birth to One.
One gives birth to Two.
Two gives birth to Three.
Three gives birth to all things.

All things have their backs to the female
and stand facing the male.
When male and female combine,
all things achieve harmony.

Ordinary men hate solitude.
But the Master makes use of it,
embracing his aloneness, realizing
he is one with the whole universe.

The Tao is beyond distinctions.

Everything we see and distinguish is part of Oneness/Wholeness. It's all part of the Tao. If you like, the Tao is the origin of everything. We may recall, "The Tao is called the Great Mother: empty yet inexhaustible, it gives birth to infinite worlds" (chapter 6). The Tao is also where everything returns to. "All things end in the Tao as rivers flow into the sea" (chapter 32).

From our perspective, our life is what happens in the meantime. And while we are alive, our minds like to separate and distinguish things. We do this by naming them. Naming is what separates things out from Oneness/Wholeness, which is, of course, unnamable. Thus "the unnamable is the eternally real. Naming is the origin of all particular things" (chapter 1).

So here's an example. "One." As soon as we start, then all the rest follows. "One gives birth to Two. Two gives birth to Three. Three gives birth to all things." So there we have it. Now we have populated our world with particular things. And our minds are now content as we sift and sort through our world, classifying things, forming opinions about them, judging them, having desires about them; even seeing ourselves as one of them.

Note that there is nothing wrong with this process as long as we don't kid ourselves by expecting to find unity and harmony among the pieces. We won't. Unity and harmony lie only at the level of Oneness/Wholeness. And we have to stand back, far back, to see this.

Let's illustrate this with one of our distinctions. Pick one. It doesn't matter which. Let's pick male and female. Now imagine a straight line. Put male at one end of it and female at the other. Now stand yourself in the middle. So which way will you face? You have to face one way or the other, because you cannot face both ways. So pick one. It doesn't matter which. Have you made your choice? Okay. It looks like you now have your back to the female and are facing the male. That's fine. Maybe others would have done the same. If so, the result would be that "all things have their backs to the female and stand facing the male." This example is just an illustration.

So here's the test question: Have you achieved harmony? And the answer is no, you have merely created separation and distinction. This is fine, as long as you weren't expecting anything else. Harmony lies only at the level where there is no distinction. You have to combine everything together again to achieve this. "When male and female combine, all things achieve harmony."

So, if making distinctions is not the way to go, then how can you achieve harmony? As we said, you now have to stand back, far back. One way to do this is to remove yourself from the world of distinctions. How? Solitude. Just be alone. Most people don't like to do this, for fear of leaving their familiar world. But aloneness is nothing to be feared. Indeed it's the simplest way to lose thoughts of separation and distinction and reconnect yourself with Oneness/Wholeness. This is what the Master does. "Ordinary men hate solitude. But the Master makes use of it, embracing his aloneness, realizing he is one with the whole universe."

In solitude your mind can be quiet. Distinctions can stop. Everything becomes clean and simple. "Express yourself completely, then keep quiet. Be like the forces of nature: when it blows, there is only wind; when it rains, there is only rain; when the clouds pass, the sun shines through" (chapter 23). This is what achieving harmony looks like. Except you don't need the words.

How seldom we leave our familiar world populated with all the distinctions of which we are typically so proud. How comfortable and at home we feel in it. Why would we go anywhere else?

Have you ever embraced solitude? Not just happened to find yourself alone, but deliberately gone out of your way to be alone? And when you have done this, have you noticed that comments, opinions, labels all fall away? They have no meaning if there's no one else to hear them. The beauty of solitude is that you therefore don't make the comment, you don't form the opinion, and you don't label and point things out, because there's no one else there. It's just you alone with what is.

This chapter reminds us that when we embrace aloneness, all distinctions fall away. What remains is oneness. It is then that we realize it includes us. We are not distinct. Rather, we are "one with the whole universe."

43

The gentlest thing in the world
overcomes the hardest thing in the world.
That which has no substance
enters where there is no space.
This shows the value of non-action.

Teaching without words,
performing without actions:
that is the Master's way.

Moving beyond words and actions.

When you dwell in harmony with the Tao, your actions are naturally aligned with it and you succeed without trying. When we live outside the Tao, we typically think it takes effort to achieve results. As the saying goes, "If at first you don't succeed, then try, try again." So if something is hard, the way to overcome it is to try again, still harder. Most of the time, this thinking underlies our approach to everything we do.

Our sequence goes like this: desire, goal, plan, milestones, action. Ready, set, go. It's all about us and what we want to achieve and the results we (often) want to display for others to see. However, we may recall, "The Master, by residing in the Tao, sets an example for all beings. . . . He doesn't display himself. . . . Because he has no goal in mind, everything he does succeeds" (chapter 22).

Thus living in harmony with the Tao is not about goals, and our typical approach is in fact back to front. The way to overcome the hardest thing is not with force at all, but by letting go. What could be gentler than letting go? Thus "the gentlest thing in the world overcomes the hardest thing in the world." Similarly, capability to produce results comes not from being full of yourself (and your desires and goals) but from emptiness. This happens when "that which has no substance," emptiness, "enters where there is no space," fullness.

This sounds good, but exactly how does this happen? The answer is that we simply need to let it. We just need our self, with its desires and goals, to step aside and allow our inner space to be empty. The key word is "allow." We cannot force things. There is nothing we need to "do." This is the exact opposite of our typical actions. How can we describe it? Perhaps "non-action" is a good word. "This shows the value of non-action."

Only when we are empty of ourselves can we be full of the Tao. When that happens, we embody the Tao and everything we do succeeds, because our actions are in natural harmony with it. We are not separate and "trying to be" in harmony. There is no separation. We have become the Tao, if you like. Thus we succeed, paradoxically, by not trying to succeed. "Practice not-doing, and everything will fall into place" (chapter 3).

When we are full of our self, the opposite is true. There is no room for the Tao, and our actions consist of doing things to achieve goals and fulfill desires. They become means to an end rather than ends in themselves. In contrast, actions performed in harmony with the Tao are ends in themselves because they are not done to achieve goals. Acting in harmony is the goal. It doesn't matter what the action is; it's timeless. Thus "when her work is done, she forgets it. That is why it lasts forever" (chapter 2).

These are the actions we can learn from. These actions are the teaching of the Master. He does not teach with words and all the noise that goes with them. His actions speak for themselves. As the saying goes, actions speak louder than words. We may remember, "Therefore the Master acts without doing anything and teaches without saying anything" (chapter 2). Similar words are here: "Teaching without words, performing without actions: that is the Master's way."

All this is easy to say but hard to do. In fact, letting go of our self in our typical, busy, everyday lives is probably "the hardest thing in the world" for us to do!

How often we believe action is the only way to produce results. And we typically talk a lot more than we act. As they say, when all is said and done, much more is said than done.

Have you ever wondered what it was that needed to be done in the first place? And, for that matter, what it was that needed to be talked about? Much of the time, the answer has to do with satisfying desires of one sort or another. And since the world does not typically do a good job of satisfying desires, at least from our perspective, we view the world as something to be "overcome."

This chapter reminds us to focus on what lies on the other side of words and actions. Silence. Not "doing" anything in particular. Performing "non-actions," if you like. Just living in harmony with what is. "That is the Master's way."

44

Fame or integrity: which is more important?
Money or happiness: which is more valuable?
Success or failure: which is more destructive?

If you look to others for fulfillment,
you will never truly be fulfilled.
If your happiness depends on money,
you will never be happy with yourself.

Be content with what you have;
rejoice in the way things are.
When you realize there is nothing lacking,
the whole world belongs to you.

Rejoice in the way things are.

The path comes from the inside out; it does not go from the outside in. The path to peace, contentment, and serenity comes from being true to your inner self and being at one with the Tao. It is only our self that would have us think the path goes from the outside in. In other words, that our satisfaction with life all depends on what happens in the outside world. So if we are not enjoying peace, contentment, and serenity, then there are a lot of things we need to do.

For example, there are goals to be set and achieved. There are people who need to think well of us. There is money that needs to be stockpiled, and then—only then—will we be happy. It's no surprise that this isn't how it works. It's likely also no surprise that we seem to keep forgetting this. When will we learn? That's a good question. Let's see what we have learned so far, by having a quiz.

"Fame or integrity: which is more important?" Fame is not the right answer. Fame is all about what others think of us. This is not where contentment comes from. Contentment is an inside job. It comes from accepting yourself. We may remember, "Because he is content with himself, he doesn't need others' approval" (chapter 30).

Let's try another question: "Money or happiness: which is more valuable?" This is an easy one. The answer is happiness. Good, clearly we have learned something! Maybe we're remembering, "Chase after money and security and your heart will never unclench" (chapter 9). Next: "Success or failure: which is more destructive?" Ooh, this is a trick question. Because the answer is yes. Success and failure are equally destructive, because our tendency is to chase one and avoid the other and thereby fail to accept whatever is here right now.

You did pretty well on the quiz. So let's explore the answers a little more. Why is fame less important than integrity? Because fame depends on what others think of you, not on your acceptance of yourself. "If you look to others for fulfillment, you will never truly be fulfilled." Why? Because chasing the approval of others is a never-ending game in which you are always at their mercy. We may recall, "Care about people's approval and you will be their prisoner" (chapter 9). This is not the way to go.

Next: "If your happiness depends on money, you will never be happy with yourself." Why? Because you have pinned your happiness on something outside yourself that you can never have enough of. This is another doomed approach. So what's the right way to go?

The answer is simple. Turn around. Stop looking outside. Look inside. You're here. You've already arrived. There is nowhere you need to strive to get to. You don't need just a bit more money or just one more person's approval. "Be content with what you have; rejoice in the way things are." You don't need more, whatever "more" may consist of. You already have all you need. In fact, the moment "you realize there is nothing lacking," the whole world belongs to you.

So if you want happiness and fulfillment, stop chasing after things in the outside world. Stop trying to possess things for yourself. Let go of them. And while you're at it, let go of yourself. Look what the Master does. "She is detached from all things; that is why she is one with them. Because she has let go of herself, she is perfectly fulfilled" (chapter 7). Imagine what it would be like if we all did this. "People would be content with their simple, everyday lives, in harmony, and free of desire" (chapter 37). Try it and see.

How often we look outside ourselves for fulfillment. We need other people to think well of us. We need to do things in the outside world to produce money. When enough people think well of us and we have enough money, then, and only then, will we be happy. At least, that's what we think.

Have you ever wondered exactly when this might be? What if the answer were never? Needs and desires are like a bottomless pit. However much you satisfy them, you will always feel you are lacking. Others may promote you on the organizational ladder, but there is (almost) always one rung higher. You may have a fancy car or house or boat (or any other material possession), but someone somewhere has a fancier one.

This chapter reminds us that the moment we are content with what we have and rejoice in the way things are, is the moment we realize "there is nothing lacking." The moment we don't need things to belong to us is the moment the whole world belongs to us, as it were. Why? Because we are on the other side of desire. This is the place to dwell.

45

True perfection seems imperfect,
yet it is perfectly itself.
True fullness seems empty,
yet it is fully present.

True straightness seems crooked.
True wisdom seems foolish.
True art seems artless.

The Master allows things to happen.
She shapes events as they come.
She steps out of the way
and lets the Tao speak for itself.

Let the Tao speak for itself.

Reality is the Tao that simply "is" all things. Illusion is what we see with our mind's eye, with the eye of thought, which sees things as separate and makes distinctions between them. Separation is illusion. Unity is real. Obviously, thought doesn't see it this way. Why does this matter?

It matters because it means the eye of thought can never see things as they really are. It will always see them as separate and in the context of the other separate things it thinks it sees. For example, look at perfection and what do we think we see? We see it in comparison with something else. It doesn't matter what. With something that is, I don't know . . . less perfect. Thus "true perfection seems imperfect, yet it is perfectly itself."

The point is that we miss the point. The point is that perfection is what it is. It is "true" in and of itself. It is not true in relation to something else. It needs no context. We are the ones that seem to need to create a context in which to see things rather than see them simply as they are. With the eye of thought, we miss the truth every time. Thus "true straightness seems crooked. True wisdom seems foolish. True art seems artless."

Why do we do this? Because our minds like to separate reality into pieces and then seek to know and understand the pieces. The trouble is, separated out from Oneness/Wholeness, pieces have no meaning. Context is what gives them meaning. And so we create context. But who said the pieces needed "meaning" in the first place? We did. In reality, all things simply "are" as they are. They don't need to have any "meaning" associated with them. Only our minds think they do.

Why? I think our minds do this to justify their own existence. After all, what's the purpose of the mind other than to understand the world around us? And what's understanding, if not analyzing what we see into parts and then assembling them into thought structures to "explain" what we see? This is what the pursuit of knowledge is all about. Well, this noisy mental activity is all very interesting, but is it the way to dwell in the Tao? No, not really.

Dwelling in the Tao means being empty of thought, empty of desire to understand things in terms of what we so boldly think are their constituent parts. The truth is, we can never understand reality in the sense of knowing it; we can only be aware of it and accept it as it is. And awareness and knowledge are fundamentally different. One leads to reality, the other to illusion. This is a tough pill to swallow. Not surprisingly, thought simply cannot swallow it. And so, to the degree that we are our thoughts, we typically don't swallow it either. Instead, we believe that knowledge is what allows us to do deliberate things, to make things happen to fulfill our desires. And so we create the world we live in. Never mind that it's an illusion.

In contrast, to dwell in the Tao is to be full of the Tao, which is to be empty of your self; to have literally let your self go. You no longer seek to fulfill your desires, because there is no "you" to do the seeking or have the desires, for that matter. Thus "true fullness seems empty, yet it is fully present." What's missing is "you." What's present is the Tao, which you embody.

This is what the Master does. She is empty of desire, empty of thought, empty even of the thinker that's doing the thinking. She doesn't do deliberate things to make things happen. "The Master allows things to happen. She shapes events as they come." She gets herself out of the picture. She has nothing to add. There is nothing to say. "She steps out of the way and lets the Tao speak for itself."

How often we like to shape events before they come. We preconceive, we form expectations, we plan—often in great detail. Then we execute our plans. And we certainly do not "step out of the way." After all, we need to be ready to jump right in if things are not unfolding the way we want.

Have you ever truly stepped out of the way? Simply allowed things to happen on their own and been a part of them as they did? This doesn't mean you become a passive spectator. It means that instead of directing and controlling (or trying to), you allow yourself to take direction from the flow. Instead of force-fitting events to conform to your desires, you gently shape them as they come.

This chapter reminds us that only when we stop issuing instructions can we hear the Tao. The Tao doesn't need us to speak for it. It can speak for itself. It always does. The question is, do we listen?

When a country is in harmony with the Tao,
the factories make trucks and tractors.
When a country goes counter to the Tao,
warheads are stockpiled outside the cities.

There is no greater illusion than fear,
no greater wrong than preparing to defend yourself,
no greater misfortune than having an enemy.

Whoever can see through all fear
will always be safe.

Fear is an illusion.

To live in harmony with the Tao is to be free from desire to have things be anything other than the way they are. If this were always true for everyone, then "people would be content with their simple, everyday lives, in harmony, and free of desire" (chapter 37). To go about their everyday lives, people would need no more than simple, everyday things like trucks and tractors. So that's what the factories would make.

Contrast this with living "counter to the Tao" and what do we get? In a word, we get fear. We get fear that what we have right now may be lost or taken away. We get fear that what we may desire in the future may not happen or may be prevented. So we ask ourselves, who will be doing the taking away or the preventing? Well, other people, of course. And so we start to fear other people. What should we do about them? Well, we'd better defend ourselves against them. And what do we need so that we can do that? Well, we need warheads to be "stockpiled outside the cities." So the factories would make warheads instead of trucks and tractors.

The sad thing is that this is based entirely on illusion. Why? Because as soon as we step out of harmony with the Tao, we enter the world of illusion. There are at least three illusions at work, and each is greater than the previous one. First is the illusion of thought or, more accurately, the illusion that anything that thought creates is real. Second is the illusion of desire. Desire is a thought, but it is a greater, or more powerful, illusion because it distracts us from the present moment by focusing us on a future in which our desires are fulfilled. This then causes us to act out of desire.

Third is the illusion of fear, and "there is no greater illusion than fear." Why? Because what we fear is that our desires will not be fulfilled. This then causes us to act out of fear. Thus fear is based on desire, and both are based on thought. All three make up a house of cards. None of them has any substance. If there were no thought, there would be no desire and there would be no fear. There would be no illusion. There would be only what is—in other words, the Tao.

However, the trouble is that we don't believe this. We believe all three illusions are real. And once we believe they are real, they influence what we do. This in turn influences what we experience as a result of what we do. In short, the act of believing and behaving as though these illusions are real makes them so. What we believe becomes our reality.

The Master has strong words to say about fear. Not only is there "no greater illusion," but also there is "no greater wrong" and "no greater misfortune." Why? Because when we act out of fear we see people as threats and prepare to defend ourselves against them, when the reality is that other people are nothing more than other people. It's only our thinking that turns them into "enemies." Our actions will then reflect our thinking, and soon enough we will likely turn them into real enemies through our attitudes, through how we see them, and through what we do. Sooner or later conflict will result and we will then feel our initial fears were justified. But, of course, it didn't need to be this way! We made it so.

What if we were simply to accept what is, without either desire or fear? Neither desiring it to be different and acting to make it so, nor fearing that it might be changed and acting to defend it against an imaginary enemy? Fear is our creation, an artifact of the mind, and we can see right through it any time we want. "Whoever can see through all fear will always be safe." The result would be harmony with the Tao. Is it really up to us? Yes, it is.

How often we act out of fear. Fear that we won't have enough of something. Or fear that what we have will be taken away. And then we let this fear direct our actions. Or, if we don't do this for ourselves, sometimes we believe others who tell us we have enemies and we should fear what they might do.

Have you ever wondered whether we create enemies where none exist? Have you ever wondered whether others tell us we have enemies so they can control what we do? Have you ever thought about how what we believe becomes our reality regardless of whether or not it is an illusion?

This chapter reminds us that to dwell in the Tao is to stay acutely aware, ready to see through illusion every time it appears. "Whoever can see through all fear will always be safe." Why are we safe? Because to see through fear is to realize there is nothing on the other side. Fear is the illusion. On the other side there is nothing. How can we be afraid of nothing?

47

Without opening your door,
you can open your heart to the world.
Without looking out your window,
you can see the essence of the Tao.

The more you know,
the less you understand.

The Master arrives without leaving,
sees the light without looking,
achieves without doing a thing.

Open your heart to the Tao.

Whenever we seek something, our standard approach is to assume it's "out there" somewhere. Wherever it is, it's not where we are. So we assume we have to go and get it. We have to make plans, undertake a journey, and do things to close the gap between where we are and wherever it is. At the end of the journey, we will "arrive" and claim whatever it is for ourselves and finally possess the object of our desire.

This approach might work for some objects, some of the time. However, it's not usually the objects we're after. What we really desire is the peace of mind, happiness, or serenity that we think possessing the objects will bring. Good examples are money and security. Unfortunately, what happens is that achieving the object of desire typically brings a fleeting moment of satisfaction before we discover that we now desire "more." And so the cycle continues, with peace and serenity ever beyond our grasp.

Living in harmony with the Tao is not like that. For a start, the Tao is not "out there" somewhere, there is no journey for you to undertake, and you will never arrive somewhere to claim and finally possess the Tao for yourself. What does this mean? Well, among other things, it means the standard approach is not the way to go.

Why not? The short answer is that you have already arrived, whether you know it or not. And, as a matter of fact, you cannot "know" it. Nor can you see it, grasp it, or possess it like an object. But you can open your heart to it and dwell in harmony with it. And you can do this without going anywhere. "Without opening your door, you can open your heart to the world." And here's what happens: the moment you do this, you find the peace and serenity you were looking for. "Without looking out your window, you can see the essence of the Tao." The Tao doesn't lie outside somewhere. It lies within. And you're already there.

Why is this so hard to understand? The answer is that we think about it too much. In fact, thinking about it at all is thinking too much, because the Tao can never be understood with thought. Thought can get a handle on something only if it's "out there" and can be identified, analyzed, and neatly slotted into the correct pigeonhole in the structure of knowledge. Analysis requires separateness from what is analyzed. It works only on things that are out there.

What if there is no separateness? What if the only reality is Oneness/Wholeness that cannot be split up into convenient thought-sized pieces? What if what we want to understand is not out there but lies within? Well, in that case we're stuck. We can't handle it, we can't know it, and we can't understand it. This is precisely what happens when we seek to understand the Tao. "The more you know, the less you understand." Is this a problem? Fortunately the answer is no.

Knowing and understanding the Tao is not the same as dwelling in it. And you can dwell in harmony with the Tao the moment you silence your mind and stop trying to understand the Tao with thought. Thought is illusion. So is separateness. Reality is Oneness/Wholeness. In reality there is nowhere to go other than where you are. To dwell in harmony with the Tao is to become aware that you have already arrived. You don't need to leave where you are, go looking for something, and do things along the way. Thus "the Master arrives without leaving, sees the light without looking, achieves without doing a thing." Reality is right here, right now. You're it. Don't think about it. Just be it.

How often we look out our window, as it were, expecting to see the Tao somewhere else. We believe we need to go out our door, as it were, and undertake a journey to get from here to there. And when we don't understand something, we believe the only way is to acquire more knowledge.

It's true that knowledge can answer many questions. But have you ever noticed that on the tail of every answer lies another question, and then another and another? All this is fine on a superficial level. After all, knowledge has its uses. But the pursuit of knowledge is all on the other side of the window. What if the light that underlies everything is not on the other side of the window? And what if instead of opening your door, you opened your heart?

This chapter reminds us that the light is not outside, it's inside. And it's there all the time. You don't need to go anywhere. It's under your feet. Stay at the center, rooted in the Tao, and it will be as if your actions become effortless. You will achieve "without doing a thing."

48

In the pursuit of knowledge,
every day something is added.
In the practice of the Tao,
every day something is dropped.
Less and less do you need to force things,
until finally you arrive at non-action.
When nothing is done,
nothing is left undone.

True mastery can be gained
by letting things go their own way.
It can't be gained by interfering.

Knowledge often gets in the way.

The pursuit of knowledge works like this: The human mind seeks to understand and believes the way to do so is to analyze what's out there with thought. This is a big undertaking, because there's a lot out there. We start by identifying and naming things and then build relationships between them to connect them all together again into a structure that we call knowledge.

There's nothing wrong with this. Knowledge can be very useful. Thoughts about things can be tested and proved to be true or false. Science works by accepting as solid building blocks only the hypotheses that have withstood tests to disprove them. It's all very organized with rules, laws, and principles. And so the structure of knowledge grows and grows. "In the pursuit of knowledge, every day something is added."

Is this a useful exercise? Sure it is. Along the way we can use our knowledge to predict and control certain aspects of our natural world. We can dam rivers and create hydroelectricity, we can repair damage to the human body and prevent illness, and we can send a man to the moon and listen to the stars with radio telescopes. All very impressive.

Will we ever know all there is to be known? No, we won't. Will we keep pursuing knowledge as long as our inquiring minds are active? Yes, we will. After all, it's a big undertaking. Talk to any scientist. Before we can push back the frontiers of knowledge, we have to study what's already known, to prove we're on the frontier. Only then can we "boldly go where no man has gone before." It's a noble pursuit. But it's a pursuit nonetheless, and one without an end.

Contrast this with the practice of the Tao. There is no pursuit. There is no "end." If you like the image of an end, then the end is the beginning. If you like the image of a journey, then you arrive without leaving. But the mind has a tough time digesting these phrases, because when you think about them they don't make sense. They aren't solid building blocks that can be incorporated into the structure of knowledge. But what if they're true nonetheless?

To practice the Tao is to be aware and accept what "is" and to dwell in harmony with it. Oddly enough, this doesn't call for an understanding of the structure of knowledge. Nor does it call for you to do any "thing." At the end of the day, "things" don't really need you to help them "go their own way." They can get there just fine without you. Not to be unkind, but your attempts to help them along are most likely done with fulfilling your desires in mind and thus amount to "interfering."

So how do you achieve this awareness? Not with the machinery of thought. If anything, the practice of the Tao calls for methodically removing the thoughts that block your awareness. "In the practice of the Tao, every day something is dropped." Another block falls away. "Less and less do you need to force things" into the structure of preexisting knowledge.

But isn't this just another endless pursuit? No, because you arrive the moment you realize there is no "thing" that you need to do. Everything is perfect just the way it is. Does this mean you don't matter? That you can't make a difference? That you now do nothing? Absolutely not.

If you like, think of the universe as music all around you. Your job is to discover your song and sing it in harmony. Singing is not doing nothing. Nor is it interfering. It is singing. Being part of the Tao is about being. It is not about doing things. "When nothing is done, nothing is left undone." Being, not doing—this is "true mastery."

How often we believe that more knowledge is the answer to everything. The way to understand something is to analyze it, study the (so-called) constituent parts, and then try to understand the world in terms of them. And there is nothing wrong with this. Often it works. As we have seen, the pursuit of knowledge has many useful applications. The trouble starts when we confuse what we know with everything there is and believe knowledge alone should guide all our actions.

Have you ever simply let things go their own way and been surprised at how well they worked out? Perhaps you have done this for things you felt didn't matter too much. But what about bigger things? What if you were to act from awareness rather than from what we call knowledge? This is an unnerving thought, isn't it? But the keyword is "thought." What if, in some cases, thought and knowledge were not the solution but part of the problem? Perhaps even the whole problem?

This chapter reminds us that living in the Tao is a practice, not a pursuit. And it involves letting go of what we think we know. When we trust ourselves to the Tao, we act from beyond thought and knowledge. And when we do, we find that nothing needs to be forced. No interfering is needed. In fact, we don't need to "do" anything in particular. Our actions simply become part of the flow. And so we become part of the flow.

49

The Master has no mind of her own.
She works with the mind of the people.

She is good to people who are good.
She is also good to people who aren't good.
This is true goodness.

She trusts people who are trustworthy.
She also trusts people who aren't trustworthy.
This is true trust.

The Master's mind is like space.
People don't understand her.
They look to her and wait.
She treats them like her own children.

Keep your mind open.

To act in harmony with the Tao is to have nothing "in mind." Thus the Master has no desires, no agenda. She's not seeking to gain anything or to interfere with anything. "The Master has no mind of her own." But she is alive and present and capable of acting in harmony with the Tao. So how does she interact with other people?

Typically, when we "do things," we have fulfillment of some desire in mind. So the best way to work with us is to get inside our head. That will tell you where we're coming from and where we think we're going. Note that when we do things to satisfy desire, there is always judgment. An action is good if it serves as a means to an end, and bad if it doesn't. And we typically apply the same judgment to people. So if you want to work with us, then this is what we have "in mind." This is what the Master has to deal with when "she works with the mind of the people."

But when the Master interacts with others she is coming from a different place. Acting in harmony with the Tao and acting to fulfill desire are fundamentally different. When there is no desire, there is no judgment. When there is no judgment, there is only compassion. Thus the Master behaves the same way toward all people. She is good to them and she trusts them regardless of where they're coming from. "She is good to people who are good. She is also good to people who aren't good." "She trusts people who are trustworthy. She also trusts people who aren't trustworthy." It makes no difference to her.

Doesn't this make her a little naive? Might not bad and untrustworthy people take advantage of her? Yes, there's a possibility they might. But the point is that it doesn't influence what she does. Acting in harmony with the Tao never depends on what someone else might or might not do. If it did, we would have to look inside our mind to determine how to act. We would have to make judgments about others, label them good or bad, and then second-guess what they might or might not do before we did whatever it was we were about to do. Our minds would be full.

In contrast, the Master's mind is empty. "The Master's mind is like space." No preconceptions, no judgments; just awareness. If we could get inside her mind, we wouldn't find anything there. As a result, we cannot tell where she's coming from. This is why "people don't understand her." She is good to people and trusts people regardless of judgments about their goodness or trustworthiness. She's coming from a place beyond goodness and trust. She's coming from a place that's beyond labels. She's coming from the Tao. "This is true goodness." "This is true trust." And it really doesn't need a label at all. It just is.

So if the Master works with the mind of the people, then how do they work with her? Does the process work the same way? No, it doesn't. People find they cannot ascribe desires to her, so they cannot second-guess her, and they cannot tell where she's coming from. As a result, all they can do is "look to her and wait," presumably to see if she's good and/or trustworthy.

In contrast, the Master doesn't have to wait. She doesn't know where other people are coming from either, but the difference is that she doesn't need to know. Why? Because she's going to treat them all with the same compassion. "She treats them like her own children."

How often we do not trust and instead treat others with suspicion. We think we need to watch them and label them good or bad before we decide how we should act toward them.

Have you ever met someone who accepted you just the way you were? Of course you have. They didn't second-guess where you were coming from, what your motives might be, and whether they might be good or bad. We sometimes talk about letting down our defenses. Have you ever wondered why they should be up in the first place?

This chapter reminds us that true goodness and true trust are not conditional on anything. We do not need to look inside our own minds to take direction from our judgments of and labels for the outside world. Instead, when our minds are empty "like space," our actions can spring from compassion, with nothing in the way.

50

The Master gives himself up
to whatever the moment brings.
He knows that he is going to die,
and he has nothing left to hold on to:
no illusions in his mind,
no resistances in his body.
He doesn't think about his actions;
they flow from the core of his being.
He holds nothing back from life;
therefore he is ready for death,
as a man is ready for sleep
after a good day's work.

Hold nothing back.

This chapter is about letting go. This is very hard for us to do.

Typically, we act with intent to fulfill desire. Desire is always rooted in the self. In other words, what we want for our "self" is the motive behind what we do. And we see each moment as raw material to be used as a means to this end. In this respect, we are full of ourselves. In contrast, the Master desires nothing and is empty of himself. His actions are not a means to an end; each moment exists for him to go with the flow. "The Master gives himself up to whatever the moment brings."

We tend to live with our life in mind and "hold on" to our desires, plans, and thoughts. Why? Because we typically use the extent to which we satisfy our desires as the measure of our success and happiness. So desires, plans, and thoughts are very important to us. We're generally not interested in "whatever the moment brings," except to the extent that it suits our purposes. If it doesn't, then we will meet it with resistance and see if we can bend it to meet our desires.

Needless to say, this is not how to live in harmony with the Tao. In the Tao, reality is Oneness/Wholeness. Everything else is illusion. Thought is illusion because it separates and divides Oneness/Wholeness into separate named pieces. The pieces are illusions because they're artifacts of the mind. Desire involves chasing after the pieces, so it's illusion too. In fact, so is the self that is doing the thinking and desiring. It's all illusion.

So how do you act in harmony with the Tao? How do you live in reality as opposed to illusion? Try this. What if you lived with your death in mind rather than your life? Of all the things you worry about and desire and make plans to acquire, how many of them will you take with you when you die? None of them, right? So why "hold on" to them while you're alive? Why let them exert such influence over what you do during the brief period of time in which you live? Why resist "whatever the moment brings" and view it only as a means to an end? What if living in the moment were an end in itself?

This is what the Master does. He lives with his death in mind. "He knows that he is going to die." He has unbundled himself from thought and desire. He knows "he has nothing left to hold on to: no illusions in his mind, no resistances in his body." Like us, the Master acts, but his actions bypass the mind completely. "He doesn't think about his actions; they flow from the core of his being." He doesn't carefully measure himself out, investing himself in life wherever he thinks he might get the best return in the future. "He holds nothing back from life." This is it. Now.

We typically live with our life in mind, not our death, because we want to keep satisfying our desires. It doesn't seem to occur to us that however much we get, we will always desire "more" and that we are the prisoners of our desires. Instead, we let our desires rob us of whatever the present moment brings, because we're too busy either worrying about the future or regretting the past. No, we're not ready for death.

Free from illusion, the Master lives entirely in the present. He "gives himself up to whatever the moment brings" because he has no need or desire to resist it. "Therefore he is ready for death, as a man is ready for sleep after a good day's work." It's all part of the flow.

How seldom we live in the present. How often we hold on to whatever we desire in our future and meet the present with resistance if it does not conform to our desires. How often we regret some aspect of the past and hold back from life for fear that something we did not like might repeat itself.

Have you ever truly given yourself up to "whatever the moment brings"? This is not easy. Nor is it easy to bypass thought and let your actions "flow from the core of [your] being." Nor is it easy to let go instead of holding on.

This chapter reminds us to trust and let go. There's a saying, "I do not fear death, I fear not having lived fully." To hold nothing back is to live fully. So to live fully is to no longer fear death. After a good day's work of living fully, we are all ready for a sleep. The same is true after a lifetime of living fully. What could be more natural than that?

51

Every being in the universe
is an expression of the Tao.
It springs into existence,
unconscious, perfect, free,
takes on a physical body,
lets circumstances complete it.
That is why every being
spontaneously honors the Tao.

The Tao gives birth to all beings,
nourishes them, maintains them,
cares for them, comforts them, protects them,
takes them back to itself,
creating without possessing,
acting without expecting,
guiding without interfering.
That is why love of the Tao
is in the very nature of things.

Everything is an expression of the Tao.

Since we have desires, one way for us to relate to the Tao is to imagine what its desires would be if it had them. If the Tao had a desire, it would be to express itself. This chapter tells us we can think of everything in the universe as "an expression of the Tao." So the Tao expresses itself and we, along with everything else in the universe, are the result.

This image helps, because it reminds us that everything comes into existence in natural harmony with the Tao. It requires no involvement of consciousness and thought. There's no need to compare things with some imagined better version of themselves and then work to make them conform to this idea. Instead, things are perfect just the way they are. Every being "springs into existence, unconscious, perfect, free."

However, our experience tells us things also change. Indeed, life consists of change. Like springing into existence, change is perfectly natural if things change at their own pace as the universe unfolds. Our thoughts and desires do not need to be the drivers. Thus anything in the universe "takes on a physical body" and "lets circumstances complete it." This is the Tao expressing itself. Our involvement is not required. We likely find this a bit humbling.

But, if you think about it, how can we know better than the Tao? Do we really know how something should be "completed"? It's really an extraordinary act of pride to presume we know best. When we swing into action with our idea of what needs to be done, nothing natural and spontaneous is about to happen. We're typically intent on getting things to meet our desires. From the perspective of the Tao, this amounts to nothing less than interfering. You could almost say it amounts to dis-honoring the Tao!

On the other hand, left alone, things are free to unfold in natural harmony. "That is why every being spontaneously honors the Tao." Our helping hands are not required. If you like, think of the Tao as a very capable set of hands for all things to be in. We're told they give birth, nourish, maintain, care for, comfort, and protect. That's a pretty good list. Has anything been left out? Oh yes, when the existence of things comes to an end, the Tao also takes them back to itself. "All things end in the Tao as rivers flow into the sea" (chapter 32). If this is the natural order of things, do we really think we can improve on it?

Our part is to relax, act in harmony with the Tao, and live in the present moment. Typically, our actions are driven by a desired future state. When we create, we want to possess the results of our creation. When we act, we have expectations in mind. All these look to the future. Contrast this with how the Tao works: "Creating without possessing, acting without expecting, guiding without interfering." All these activities are oriented in the present. And we can learn a lot from this list.

If we create, act, and guide instead of standing apart, directing, controlling, and interfering, then we become part of the natural harmony and we honor the Tao. If everything is an expression of the Tao, then it's in the nature of things, ourselves included, to unfold in harmony with it. "That is why love of the Tao is in the very nature of things." So it's in our very nature as well.

How often we think we know better. How often we regard the world around us as raw material to be directed and controlled to satisfy our desires. If something is not the way we want, we are not at all interested in letting "circumstances complete it." That's our job. We'll complete it the way we want. And we don't need any help doing it.

Have you ever found life to be a struggle and wondered why? At other times, have you ever found your life just seemed to flow almost without effort? Chances are, when it flowed you were creating without intent to possess the results, acting without preconceived expectations, and guiding without interfering. What if this experience did not depend on chance? What if it depended simply on awareness and self-mastery?

This chapter reminds us that everything is an expression of the Tao. When we struggle, it is typically because we do not trust how things are unfolding around us and have some better version in mind. We are reminded there is nothing more trustworthy than the Tao.

52

In the beginning was the Tao.
All things issue from it;
all things return to it.

To find the origin,
trace back the manifestations.
When you recognize the children
and find the mother,
you will be free of sorrow.

If you close your mind in judgments
and traffic with desires,
your heart will be troubled.
If you keep your mind from judging
and aren't led by the senses,
your heart will find peace.

Seeing into darkness is clarity.
Knowing how to yield is strength.
Use your own light
and return to the source of light.
This is called practicing eternity.

Return to the source of light.

How can we find the Tao? We can't, but we keep trying, and this tends to bring sorrow. However, is the Tao really the sort of thing we can "find"? "In the beginning was the Tao. All things issue from it; all things return to it." We may also remember, "It flows through all things, inside and outside, and returns to the origin of all things" (chapter 25). This description sounds pretty elusive. If we somehow get to the "origin," will we find the Tao there?

In reality, the answer is that we're already there, because all separation is illusion and only unity is real, which means there is no "there" to get to. But we typically don't live in this reality. Instead, we tend to live in the world of the mind, which is a world of illusion that we believe to be real. Rather than trust our natural selves, we typically trust our mind and get taken along for the ride as it separates, names, analyzes, and builds knowledge structures to connect the separate things it believes it finds "out there." And, of course, the Tao is one of those "things." It's our mind that asks how we can find the Tao and slot it neatly into the structure of knowledge.

But, before we go there, how can a search within the world of illusion possibly yield anything real? Isn't our mind-based search to find the Tao doomed from the outset? These are good questions.

Remember, we do not see reality when we're caught in the world of the mind. We see only the separate things we name. These are not real. They're artificial manifestations. We may recall, "The unnamable is the eternally real. Naming is the origin of all particular things. Free from desire, you realize the mystery. Caught in desire, you see only the manifestations" (chapter 1). But here comes the clue: "Mystery and manifestation arise from the same source. This source is called darkness. . . . The gateway to all understanding" (chapter 1). So this chapter tells us that if we want "to find the origin, trace back the manifestations."

What does this mean? It means one mind-based way to "find" the Tao is to think of your thoughts as children and keep tracing them back and back. "When you recognize the children and find the mother, you will be free of sorrow." You may recall, "There was something formless and perfect before the universe was born. It is serene. Empty. Solitary. Unchanging. Infinite. Eternally present. It is the mother of the universe. For lack of a better name, I call it the Tao" (chapter 25). There it is. The original mother is the Tao. Keep tracing back and you will eventually get there.

So there are two ways to "find" the Tao. The simpler way is to let your mind become quiet, serene, empty, and you will naturally return to the origin of all things to discover (or rediscover) that you were there all the time. Or you can work with your mind and its thoughts or manifestations and play the tracing game. Either way, when you find the mother, your mind will stop in silence as it is finally confronted with something greater than itself and realizes that it was included all along. Both ways work. The first is more direct. You pick which approach to take.

If you go the mind route, be sure to keep your mind open, stay in control, and don't get taken for a ride. Because "if you close your mind in judgments and traffic with desires, your heart will be troubled. If you keep your mind from judging and aren't led by the senses, your heart will find peace." So don't be led by your senses, don't be driven by desires, and don't judge.

But remember this is only one way. The mind will always look outward and see only darkness. A better way is to look within. "Use your own light and return to the source of light. This is called practicing eternity."

How often we believe everything starts and ends with us. Our world is typically self-centered, with us at the center looking out. We think we're looking at reality, which is outside. When we look inside all we see, at first glance, is darkness. There's no point in looking there. And yet so often our heart is troubled, we do not find peace, and we wonder why.

Have you ever looked inside for a long time? Gone into solitude until your mind stops chattering? This is hard to do, given the way we typically live our busy everyday lives. Our mind has endless opportunities to chatter. In fact, we typically find it quite unsettling when things fall silent, so we seek out stimulation of one sort or another to start the chatter again.

This chapter reminds us that peace is where the light is, which is at the center of all things. It is the Tao, not we, that is at the center. This is the place to be. If we look inside for longer than a first glance, what we'll see is not darkness but light. Why? Because we are already there. We were looking in the wrong place.

53

The great Way is easy,
yet people prefer the side paths.
Be aware when things are out of balance.
Stay centered within the Tao.

When rich speculators prosper
while farmers lose their land;
when government officials spend money
on weapons instead of cures;
when the upper class is extravagant and irresponsible
while the poor have nowhere to turn—
all this is robbery and chaos.
It is not in keeping with the Tao.

Stay centered within the Tao.

What do we have here? A political statement? It sounds like either a call to revolutionary action or a sad reflection on human nature. Of course it's neither. It's simply an observation or two, like all the other chapters in the Tao, intended to slow us down and think about how thought and desire upset the balance of the Tao. The message is "Be aware when things are out of balance." And when we find that they are, "stay centered within the Tao."

So how can we tell when things are out of balance? What follows is a list of examples. All of them involve people. Three groups take a hit here: speculators, government officials, and the upper class. Each group upsets the balance by being driven by something other than acceptance of what is, living in the present moment, and dwelling in harmony with the Tao.

Speculators, by their very nature, speculate about how a future state of affairs could bring them material profit and then act to bring that future into being. This is out of balance with the Tao in at least three ways. First, speculators are driven by a desired future state, so they immediately miss living fully in the present moment. Second, their desire is for material possessions of some sort or another, which always bring only fleeting satisfaction until they are replaced by the desire for "more." Third, their pursuit of this desire causes harm to others, in this case farmers: "when rich speculators prosper while farmers lose their land."

Next are the government officials spending public money on weapons. This is out of balance with the Tao in at least two ways. First, weapons are always a reaction to fear. "There is no greater illusion than fear, no greater wrong than preparing to defend yourself" (chapter 46). "Warheads are stockpiled outside the cities" when "a country goes counter to the Tao" (chapter 46). Second, reaction to this fear causes resources to be diverted from more worthwhile endeavors; in this case the money is spent "on weapons instead of cures." In other words, military spending means government funds are not available for health research. A timeless observation, as true today as when it was written 2,500 years ago.

The third example is the upper class acting in "extravagant and irresponsible" ways. Unlike the other two, we're not given specific examples in this case. However, the word "extravagant" implies spending more than a "responsible" amount of resources on something that presumably benefits only the upper class. This is out of balance with the Tao because, like spending money on weapons instead of cures, it means those resources are not available for more worthwhile endeavors such as helping those with less. In other words, extravagance occurs when the upper class does this type of spending "while the poor have nowhere to turn."

Do you have comments? If we want to think about it and label this state of affairs, then how about "all this is robbery and chaos." That sounds pretty accurate. However, dwelling in harmony with the Tao requires neither the thinking nor the judgment that these particular labels imply. So more neutral and judgment-free words might be "It is not in keeping with the Tao." That puts it more accurately, if mildly.

Why do people prefer these "side paths" with all the difficulties they bring? Who knows? The Master simply reflects that "the great Way is easy," but his three examples show that staying on this path is clearly not. So our part is to "be aware when things are out of balance" and "stay centered in the Tao."

How often we prefer the side paths. And we don't have to be real estate speculators, government officials, or members of the upper class to do so. We wander off the great Way every time we allow ourselves to be distracted by the pursuit of material possessions or the esteem of other people.

Have you ever wondered who benefits from the way resources get used? Clearly you don't have direct personal control over how government money gets spent. The best you can do (in a democracy) is cast your vote for whichever party you think will do the most responsible job. But resources of one sort or another flow through you every day of your life. Even if it's not money that we control, each of us gets twenty-four hours a day, regardless of who we are. Where does that time get spent and who does the spending? The answer is you do, every day, whether you like it or not.

This chapter reminds us that things are at risk of getting out of balance whenever we are not centered within the Tao. The best way to keep them in balance is simple. Just stay centered.

54

Whoever is planted in the Tao
will not be rooted up.
Whoever embraces the Tao
will not slip away.
Her name will be held in honor
from generation to generation.

Let the Tao be present in your life
and you will become genuine.
Let it be present in your family
and your family will flourish.
Let it be present in your country
and your country will be an example
to all countries in the world.
Let it be present in the universe
and the universe will sing.

How do I know this is true?
By looking inside myself.

Let the Tao be present in your life.

The first lines of this chapter imply that, if you're not planted in the Tao and embracing it, then you're in danger of being "rooted up" and "slipping away." Being rooted up by what? The short answer is, by thought and desire because, unlike the Tao, they keep changing. It is also implied that you will be forgotten by others. This is a curious observation, because dwelling in the Tao does not involve concern for whether your name "will be held in honor from generation to generation." So what is this observation doing here?

Well, we need to be careful, because I inserted the word "concern." If your actions are rooted in concern to have others hold your name in honor from generation to generation, then indeed you are not living in the Tao. You're being driven by your self-image, or ego. But you can also simply act with compassion and become who you already are, with no pretensions or desires. If this is what you're doing, then not only will you dwell in harmony the Tao, but it also happens that others will likely find you noteworthy.

Who knows, maybe they will even choose to hold your name in honor from generation to generation. Maybe they won't. Either way, you're indifferent; you'll live your life the same way regardless. What others think is irrelevant to you. You may recall a similar observation in chapter 8: "When you are content to be simply yourself and don't compare or compete, everybody will respect you." Respect is not the goal; it's a by-product.

So if we're planted in the Tao and embrace it, what can we expect? What follows is a description of what happens when the Tao is present at each of four levels: your own life, your family, your country, and the universe. In short, when the Tao is present, "you will become genuine," "your family will flourish," "your country will be an example," and "the universe will sing."

What does it mean to "become genuine"? I think it means that when the Tao is present in your life, you will act to become who you already are, that is, your true inner self. Acting to inflate your self-image is what's not genuine. Why? Because when your self-image, or ego, is in charge, you'll do whatever you think will cause others to hold your name "in honor from generation to generation," to use the current example. And this action is unlikely to be true to your inner self.

When your family is full of genuine people, it will flourish. When your country is full of flourishing families, it "will be an example to all countries in the world." When the Tao is present at the level of the universe, then "the universe will sing." It doesn't get better than this. Can we help make this happen? Absolutely.

Your part is simply to "let the Tao be present in your life." The key word is "let." Simply allow it. Set your self aside, along with the machinery of thought and desire that builds your self-image, which typically drives what you do. Don't look outward to images for direction. Nothing genuine comes from them; they're illusions. Look to the reality within. Become who you already are.

How do we know this is true? Does the outside world tell us? No. Do we analyze the world and deduce it to be true for ourselves? No. Like all truth that does not rely on mind-based distinctions between things, it lies within. This is how the Master knows. "How do I know this is true? By looking inside myself." We've heard this before "How do I know this is true? I look inside myself and see" (chapter 21). The idea here is the same. Harmony with the Tao comes from within.

How often we follow our whims and desires. And every time we do, we fail to stay rooted in the Tao. This is true every time we become distracted trying to create something artificial with our lives that we think others will admire.

Have you ever wondered how we recognize what we call "genuine" people? We instinctively know they're not trying to impress anybody. They are like the Master, for whom his actions "flow from the core of his being" (chapter 50). They let themselves be who they naturally are and express who they are with their actions.

This chapter reminds us that we don't need to *try* to do this. All we need to do is get our self-important self out of the way and "let" it happen. And it will. All on its own.

55

He who is in harmony with the Tao
is like a newborn child.
Its bones are soft, its muscles are weak,
but its grip is powerful.
It doesn't know about the union
of male and female,
yet its penis can stand erect,
so intense is its vital power.
It can scream its head off all day,
yet it never becomes hoarse,
so complete is its harmony.

The Master's power is like this.
He lets all things come and go
effortlessly, without desire.
He never expects results;
thus he is never disappointed.
He is never disappointed;
thus his spirit never grows old.

Let all things come and go.

"He who is in harmony with the Tao is like a newborn child." As we grow up we tend to become rigid. We develop habits of thought and become set in our wandering ways. We may recall, "Can you coax your mind from its wandering and keep to the original oneness? Can you let your body become supple as a newborn child's?" (chapter 10). This chapter uses the image of the newborn child again and elaborates on it with three observations.

Newborn children are powerful. They are full of vital energy. And they are in natural harmony with the Tao. The second verse then explains how they have this in common with the Master.

At first glance, we might wonder how a newborn child can be powerful if "its bones are soft, its muscles weak." Can there be power without hardness and strength? "But its grip is powerful." Curiously enough, if you've held a newborn child and felt it grip your finger, you'll know this is an accurate observation.

Similarly, at first glance, we might think, why would a penis stand erect in the absence of knowledge "about the union of male and female"? Curiously enough again, if you've looked after a newborn baby boy for any length of time, you'll know this is also true. Possibly less obviously true is the reason given, that is, "so intense is its vital power." But this example is good enough for illustrative purposes.

The last observation makes you wonder whether the writer ever had a newborn child of his own: "It can scream its head off all day . . . so complete is its harmony." Harmony? Well, never mind. The point is that whatever a newborn child does, it does with all its might, with nothing held back, and with no self-consciousness. Empty of itself, the child is therefore naturally in harmony with the Tao. In summary, it is powerful, full of vitality, and dwelling in the Tao.

How is the Master's power like this? The Master is also empty of himself and thus empty of desire. Why? Because it is the self (or more accurately the self-image, or ego) that desires to control things to suit itself and satisfy its desires. Control calls for effort, because the universe seldom arranges itself to satisfy individual egos. Effort calls for action, which then gets done with expectation of a particular outcome in mind.

But when premeditated action meets the world, the results may or may not meet expectations. When they do, we get satisfaction. When they don't, we get disappointment. It's not very complicated. And desire is always at the root of it all. Without desire, it all falls away.

Thus the Master "lets all things come and go effortlessly, without desire. He never expects results; thus he is never disappointed." Does this mean he does nothing? No, on the contrary. "Because he has no goal in mind, everything he does succeeds" (chapter 22). Why? Because, empty of himself, he is empty of desire and thus acts in natural harmony with the Tao. The only difference between him and the newborn child is that he knows what he's doing. If you like, the child acts in harmony with the Tao unconsciously, whereas the Master does so consciously. The result? "His spirit never grows old." Harmony with the Tao keeps the spirit young.

How often we do not let things come and go. Instead we do the opposite. First we label some things good and others bad. Then we try to prevent the bad things from coming, and when we experience the good things, we do not let them go. We try to hold onto them. The result is that we get in the way both times.

Have you ever been disappointed? Of course you have. You had a particular expectation in mind and when reality happened, it failed to measure up. As a result, you may think the way to avoid disappointment is to have no expectations in the first place. You may also think this amounts to not caring what happens. But this is not so.

This chapter reminds us that only when we let go of expectation and allow "all things (to) come and go" can we focus on acting in harmony with the Tao. When we do, we act from compassion. And there is no greater caring than that.

56

Those who know don't talk.
Those who talk don't know.

Close your mouth,
block off your senses,
blunt your sharpness,
untie your knots,
soften your glare,
settle your dust.
This is the primal identity.

Be like the Tao.
It can't be approached or withdrawn from,
benefited or harmed,
honored or brought into disgrace.
It gives itself up continually.
That is why it endures.

Be like the Tao.

We generally have a lot to say about knowledge. After all, there's been a huge investment in building it for a long time. First, we observe what we believe to be reality, using our minds to make distinctions between all the separate things we think we see. Then we name them and connect them together again into the structure of knowledge. Formal knowledge gets taught to us as children. Then there's the informal knowledge we inherit or acquire from others as we grow up. And then there's what we build first-hand from our own experience. All this knowledge is good, solid stuff. Certainly it is a lot to talk about. Indeed, knowledge cannot be built without talking about it.

But what exactly is it that we "know"? The answer is, certainly nothing bigger than what we can wrap our minds around. So what does that mean for bigger things? What about something bigger than all the distinctions we can ever make between all the separate things we will ever see? For example, what about the eternal Oneness/Wholeness that embraces everything? This is a good question. Are we observing it; are we part of it; are we "it"? What if the answer is yes? Then we're likely a bit stumped for words—maybe even speechless, at least for a while.

We may recall, "The more you talk of it, the less you understand" (chapter 5). This chapter puts it even more bluntly. "Those who know don't talk. Those who talk don't know." The Tao is simply too big to be captured in words. Fortunately this is not a problem except for those who would rather talk than act. The Master knows this. "The Master doesn't talk, he acts" (chapter 17). "Therefore the Master acts . . . and teaches without saying anything" (chapter 2).

So if it's not knowledge that guides the Master in his actions, is it his senses? No. These are fine for observing the outside world, but they are not a source of direction. We may recall, "The Master observes the world but trusts his inner vision" (chapter 12). Direction that's in harmony with the Tao always comes from within, from the original Oneness/Wholeness, of which you appear to be a separate, temporary part. Is there a word for this? Not really. How about "the identity that existed before the one that you personally relate to at the moment"? Well, kind of. How about "This is the primal identity"? That's a bit better. At least it's fewer words.

So what do we have to do to use this "primal identity," rather than knowledge, as the basis for action? In short, shut down our senses. The following lines spell this out in quite blunt terms. Stop talking, for a start. "Close your mouth, block off your senses." So you think you can make neat, sharp distinctions? Don't kid yourself. "Blunt your sharpness." As for your elegant structures of knowledge, all you've done is tangle yourself up in them. "Untie your knots." How about that knowledge-seeking searchlight of which you're so proud? You need to "soften your glare." And what of all the separate things you think you see, with all those elaborate connections between them? In the grand scheme of things, they're no more than mental dust. "Settle your dust."

Can you arrive at the Tao? "It can't be approached or withdrawn from." Can you possess it? There's nothing for you to possess or take, because the Tao "gives itself up continually." It doesn't care what you think or don't think of it. You cannot "do" anything to it. It cannot be "benefited or harmed, honored or brought into disgrace." It's not merely bigger than you and your mind; it's beyond whatever you think space and time are. It simply is and always has been. "That is why it endures."

How often we think we know it all. And how often we talk about what we know, usually at great length, if given a chance. We think we are full of knowledge, but what we are really full of is our self. When we are full of our self, there is no room for the Tao.

Have you ever emptied your "self" to make room for the Tao? When you do this, what do you find? You find you fall silent. You join the ranks of those who know and don't talk. You may wonder why they don't talk. The answer is not because they can't. It's because, at the level of the Tao, there is nothing to be said. For those who know and don't talk, their actions are their words. And, as they say, actions speak louder.

This chapter reminds us, don't talk, and don't trust your senses. In fact, don't "do" anything. Just "be like the Tao." The less said, the better.

57

If you want to be a great leader,
you must learn to follow the Tao.
Stop trying to control.
Let go of fixed plans and concepts,
and the world will govern itself.

The more prohibitions you have,
the less virtuous people will be.
The more weapons you have,
the less secure people will be.
The more subsidies you have,
the less self-reliant people will be.

Therefore the Master says:
I let go of the law,
and people become honest.
I let go of economics,
and people become prosperous.
I let go of religion,
and people become serene.
I let go of all desire for the common good,
and the good becomes common as grass.

Learn to follow the Tao.

How do you learn to follow the Tao? All you need do is two things: "stop trying to control" and "let go." This is hard, because we tend to let ourselves and our desires get in the way. We typically attach a lot of importance to ourselves and our "fixed plans and concepts" for the way we think things ought to be.

For example, suppose we want to be "a great leader." We want to govern and have people be virtuous, secure, and self-reliant. What do we need to do? If we're motivated by desire to be seen as "a great leader," then not only do we have to do things to bring about virtue, security, and self-reliance, we also need to ensure people associate the things we do with us. Otherwise how will people recognize us as the great leader that we are? After all, our desire is not solely for virtue, security, and self-reliance for the people, it's also to be seen as a great leader. All the above is also a means to this end. It's really about us.

What does this picture look like if it's not about us? This chapter opens, "If you want to be a great leader, you must learn to follow the Tao." Will this cause people to see us as a great leader? We may recall, "When the Master governs, the people are hardly aware that he exists" (chapter 17). So the short answer is no. Dwelling in harmony with the Tao is an end in itself. It does not involve ulterior motives.

What's more, when we seek to control the world, not only do we fail in the long term but our attempts also backfire in the short term. For example, we may think the way to control people into being virtuous, secure, and self-reliant is to impose prohibitions, amass weapons, and try to alter their behavior through subsidies. But the more we do these things, "the less virtuous people will be," "the less secure," and "the less self-reliant." This is exactly what we don't want. The common theme is our lack of trust that a natural harmony exists. Do we believe the earlier sentence "Let go of fixed plans and concepts, and the world will govern itself"? Not a chance. The world couldn't possibly govern itself without us. Or so we think.

But let's look at what the Master does. For every attempt to control, what he does is "let go." And does the world fall into chaos? On the contrary. "I let go of the law, and people become honest." Note that he does not say, "I desire people to become honest and therefore I let go of the law," as though letting go of the law were a means to an end. The pattern is "I let go . . . and . . ." "I let go of economics, and people become prosperous." "I let go of religion, and people become serene." The common theme is trust. The message is, whatever you want, let go of your desire for it and allow it to spring naturally into being. "I let go of desire for the common good, and the good becomes common as grass." All on its own. No thanks to you.

What does this mean for your goal to be seen as a great leader? Well, it's not very promising. But does it really matter? No, because in the end it's about being aware of the natural harmony of the Tao and dwelling in it instead of interfering with it. When you do this, it no longer matters how you are seen by others; the "you" disappears. "The Master doesn't talk, he acts. When his work is done, the people say, 'Amazing: we did it, all by ourselves!'" (chapter 17).

Paradoxically, the best way to be remembered is to simply let go of your desire for it. "When you are content to be simply yourself . . . everybody will respect you" (chapter 8). Who knows, maybe they will even see you as "a great leader." Not that you will care, one way or the other.

How often we care about how we think we are seen. And how often this underlies and motivates what we do. Also, how often we cling to our "fixed plans and concepts" and try to control the world to make them happen.

Have you ever noticed how pervasive are our attempts to control one another and the world around us? This chapter gives the examples of law, economics, and religion. It is not hard to see how each one of these is an attempt at control. The law is the most obvious, but the other two are subtle and not-so-subtle attempts at the same thing. And there are many more.

This chapter reminds us that the Tao expresses itself best when we simply let go. So if we are leaders and want others to follow, then there is only one thing we ourselves should do, and that is "learn to follow the Tao." And we don't need to be great leaders to do that.

58

If a country is governed with tolerance,
the people are comfortable and honest.
If a country is governed with repression,
the people are depressed and crafty.

When the will to power is in charge,
the higher the ideals, the lower the results.
Try to make people happy,
and you lay the groundwork for misery.
Try to make people moral,
and you lay the groundwork for vice.

Thus the Master is content
to serve as an example
and not to impose her will.
She is pointed, but doesn't pierce.
Straightforward, but supple.
Radiant, but easy on the eyes.

Beware the will to power.

This chapter continues the theme of the last one, namely that the way to follow the Tao is to "stop trying to control" and to "let go" (chapter 57). This allows the natural harmony of the Tao to express itself without our interference. Again, the example in this chapter is government.

Our desire to control takes many forms, especially with respect to governing people. Lofty ideals such as holiness and wisdom, noble concepts such as morality and justice, practical enforcement structures such as the law—all of these represent the desire to control in action. And we don't need any of them to live in harmony with the Tao. We just need to step aside, get ourselves and our desires out of the way, and let the Tao express itself. We may recall, "Throw away holiness and wisdom, and people will be a hundred times happier. Throw away morality and justice, and people will do the right thing" (chapter 19). The same thinking is here. "If a country is governed with tolerance, the people are comfortable and honest."

Again, echoing the last chapter, we are warned that not only will our attempts to control fail in the long term, but they will also backfire in the short term. "If a country is governed with repression, the people are depressed and crafty." This is not what we had in mind at all.

What causes this? The answer is, "the will to power," which is based on either desire or fear. In the last chapter it was the desire to be seen as "a great leader." But "when the will to power is in charge, the higher the ideals, the lower the results." For example, "Try to make people happy, and you lay the groundwork for misery. Try to make people moral, and you lay the groundwork for vice." When the will to power is the driver, we're going to fail every time. Even if we don't do so immediately, we will have laid "the groundwork" for failure down the line.

Why? Because the will to power knows only one way to get what it wants, and that is to "try." In other words, to expend premeditated effort with a particular goal and expectation in mind. The last chapter observed, "I let go of the law, and people become honest" (chapter 57). Letting go is the exact opposite of trying. And it confounds the mind every time.

The Master understands this. So she does "not impose her will." She knows that "trying to dominate events goes against the current of the Tao" (chapter 30). So instead she "is content to serve as an example." How does she do this? At a high level, simply by dwelling in the Tao. "The Master, by residing in the Tao, sets an example for all beings" (chapter 22).

More specifically, "She is pointed, but doesn't pierce." She sees things as they are but is not rigid in her responses and actions. Thus she is "straightforward, but supple." While she shines, she does not dazzle with intent to impress others. You may recall the reminder to "soften your glare" (chapter 56). Here the Master is described as "radiant, but easy on the eyes."

And where does her radiance come from? In a nutshell, from following the Tao, which is to say, from not trying to control and from letting go. We may recall, "The Master keeps her mind always at one with the Tao; that is what gives her her radiance" (chapter 21). And you will shine if you do the same. "If you accept the world, the Tao will be luminous inside you" (chapter 28).

How often we let the will to power direct what we do. We claim lofty ideals and goals, but we act with anything but tolerance. We are typically intent on one thing only, and that is to impose our will. Serving as an example does not even occur to us.

Have you ever been inspired by a great leader? Have you ever wondered why that leader inspired you? Great leaders may speak fine words, but there's something about them that is beyond words. Who they are shines through in everything they do. There's a saying that leadership is example. That's the part that's inspiring you.

This chapter reminds us that lofty ideals and goals never justify the will to power. The end never justifies the means. The only way to achieve your lofty ideals and goals is to live them out in your own life. If you live in harmony with the Tao, the light will shine through you and others will notice. You will end up serving as an example whether you like it or not.

For governing a country well
there is nothing better than moderation.

The mark of a moderate man
is freedom from his own ideas.
Tolerant like the sky,
all-pervading like sunlight,
firm like a mountain,
supple like a tree in the wind,
he has no destination in view
and makes use of anything
life happens to bring his way.

Nothing is impossible for him.
Because he has let go,
he can care for the people's welfare
as a mother cares for her child.

Let go of your own ideas.

This chapter continues the theme of the last two, namely that the way to follow the Tao is to "stop trying to control" and to "let go" (chapter 57). The last chapter observed what happens when "a country is governed with tolerance" (chapter 58). This chapter continues with the similar topic of moderation, the best approach "for governing a country well."

Moderation is easy to talk about, but how would we recognize a moderate person if we saw one? The last chapter gave us a clue in that "the Master is content to serve as an example and not to impose her will." This chapter takes it one step further: "The mark of a moderate man is freedom from his own ideas."

What's wrong with ideas? Nothing. It all depends what they are and how we act on them. We need to be careful, because ideas always precede the imposing of will, which always amounts to "trying to control." This amounts to not "letting go," not allowing the natural harmony of the Tao to express itself without our interference. Ideas that precede efforts to control things are always our ideas about the way we think things ought to be. And it's when we act on them and start to impose our will that we interfere and upset the balance of the Tao.

Is there such a thing as action that is free from ideas? Yes, indeed. Just look at nature. We may recall, "Be like the forces of nature: when it blows there is only wind; when it rains, there is only rain; when the clouds pass, the sun shines through" (chapter 23). This is what freedom from ideas looks like—pure action in natural harmony with the Tao. Open, empty, anything is possible. Thus instead of imposing his will, the Master is "tolerant like the sky" and "all-pervading like sunlight." Does that mean he will get blown about by circumstance? Not at all. He is "firm like a mountain, supple like a tree in the wind."

A mind full of its own ideas cannot be open. Openness comes from freedom. We may recall, "A good scientist has freed himself of concepts and keeps his mind open to what is" (chapter 27). Locked in ideas about the way things ought to be, we are like travelers with a particular destination in mind and a fixed idea about how to get there. We think some things are useful and others aren't. So we pick and choose. We are closed to anything that doesn't help us achieve our goal. It seems we've forgotten that "a good traveler has no fixed plans and is not intent upon arriving" (chapter 27).

The moment we let go of our fixed plans, we become open to the Tao and it is ours to use. "If you open yourself to insight, you are at one with insight, and you can use it completely" (chapter 23). Suddenly we don't need to pick and choose; we can use everything, and nothing is impossible. The Master "has no destination in view and makes use of anything life happens to bring his way." And what is the consequence? "Nothing is impossible for him."

Also, when we're full of our ideas of the way things ought to be, there's no room for anything else. We view other people as no more than a means to our end. Free from our ideas, there is now room to view others with compassion. Compassion cannot be crammed into a full mind. We have to let go first. This is what the Master does. "Because he has let go, he can care for the people's welfare as a mother cares for her child."

In summary, stop trying to control, let go, be free of your own ideas, make room for compassion. Now you can dwell in harmony with the Tao, using anything life happens to bring your way.

How often we live in the world of our own ideas. We see everything through the lens of thought. And we give no thought to how much the lens might distort the reality we think we're looking at. As far as we're concerned, the way we see it is the way it is. Often we have a particular destination in view and we see only one way to get there. This description doesn't sound like the mark of a moderate man, does it?

Have you ever started on a journey only to discover a better path along the way? A rigid mind might complain that things are not going according to plan, but you can tell as a traveler that what is unfolding is better than any plan. What if you surrendered to the journey and let go of your plan entirely, simply acting with compassion to guide and shape things as they come and go?

This chapter reminds us that to do this is to live in harmony with the Tao. Instead of being rigid we become "supple like a tree in the wind." As a result, the Tao can shine through us, "all-pervading like sunlight." Why? Because we are not in the way.

———60———

Governing a large country
is like frying a small fish.
You spoil it with too much poking.

Center your country in the Tao
and evil will have no power.
Not that it isn't there,
but you'll be able to step out of its way.

Give evil nothing to oppose
and it will disappear by itself.

Give evil nothing to oppose.

Frying a small fish. What a great image for governing a large country! But what's the connection? "You spoil it with too much poking." How does "poking" connect frying a fish with governing a country?

The reason you might poke a frying fish is to make sure it's cooking evenly and not getting burned on one side. If you poked too hard and the fish was too small, then you'd likely "spoil" it by accidentally breaking it into pieces. This is not what the chef wants.

But what does "poking" look like with respect to governing a country? It looks like imposing your will because, deep down, you don't really believe that if you "let go of fixed plans and concepts . . . the world will govern itself" (chapter 57). So you start poking and trying to control and interfering. And what happens? Your efforts produce exactly what you didn't want, the same way the fish got spoiled.

Chapter 57 gave us three examples of poking followed by spoiling: prohibitions, weapons, and subsidies. "The more prohibitions you have, the less virtuous people will be. The more weapons you have, the less secure people will be. The more subsidies you have, the less self-reliant people will be." Here's another example of poking followed by spoiling: "If you don't trust the people, you make them untrustworthy" (chapter 17).

All these examples have one thing in common: lack of trust in the natural harmony of the Tao. The sole act of government should be to maintain this harmony, or restore it if it's out of balance. We may recall, "If powerful men and women could remain centered in the Tao, all things would be in harmony. The world would become a paradise. All people would be at peace, and the law would be written in their hearts" (chapter 32). No law enforcement would be needed. No poking would be required, as it were. This chapter echoes the same idea. "Center your country in the Tao and evil will have no power."

And how do you do this? In short, by not interfering. "The Master allows things to happen. She shapes events as they come. She steps out of the way and lets the Tao speak for itself" (chapter 45). Harmony can never be forced, because there will always be pushback. We may recall, "Whoever relies on the Tao in governing men doesn't try to force issues or defeat enemies by force of arms. For every force there is a counterforce," and the use of force "always rebounds upon oneself" (chapter 30).

Think of evil as a counterforce to your force. By opposing it with force, you give it strength, which rebounds on you. Can you get rid of evil? No, but you can prevent it from upsetting the balance. Simply stay centered in the Tao and, instead of opposing evil, "you'll be able to step out of its way." And what happens? "Give evil nothing to oppose and it will disappear by itself."

We may recall, "The Tao never does anything, yet through it all things are done. If powerful men and women could center themselves in it, the whole world would be transformed by itself, in its natural rhythms" (chapter 37). The natural harmony is already there and can express itself if we but "step out of its way."

Now, if the chef stepped out of the kitchen, would the small fish fry itself to perfection? Well, maybe not.

How often we poke at the world. Whatever it is we're dealing with, it's not the way we want it to be—so we poke at it. Of course, we don't call it poking. Sometimes we claim lofty ideals and give them impressive names like morality and justice. Other times we simply want to rearrange the world to better satisfy our desires. And, if we're honest, we claim nothing more lofty than that. And then the struggle begins as we seek to impose our will.

Have you ever noticed what happens when you accept the world as it is? Nothing can oppose you when you provide no opposition.

This chapter reminds us, "Give evil nothing to oppose and it will disappear all by itself." And all we have to do to step out of evil's way is remain centered in the Tao. At the center there is no struggle.

61

When a country obtains great power,
it becomes like the sea:
all streams run downward into it.
The more powerful it grows,
the greater the need for humility.
Humility means trusting the Tao,
thus never needing to be defensive.

A great nation is like a great man:
When he makes a mistake, he realizes it.
Having realized it, he admits it.
Having admitted it, he corrects it.
He considers those who point out his faults
as his most benevolent teachers.
He thinks of his enemy
as the shadow that he himself casts.

If a nation is centered in the Tao,
if it nourishes its own people
and doesn't meddle in the affairs of others,
it will be a light to all nations in the world.

Trust the Tao.

Power is an awesome responsibility, because with it comes the ability to influence the lives of others. As power grows, depending on how it's used, more people come under its influence. This is true both at the level of the individual and at the level of an entire country. "When a country obtains great power, it becomes like the sea: all streams run downward into it."

The question is, how do we use that power? At a high level, there are only two choices. One way is to use power as the means for imposing one's will. This is pride in action, either wading in, thinking it knows best or simply rearranging the world to satisfy its desires. With this approach comes fear that others will take away the objects of our desire. Thus we begin to see others as enemies and we prepare our defenses.

The other way is to step aside and allow things to unfold in natural harmony with the Tao. We limit our action to staying centered in the Tao and, if necessary, acting with compassion to restore balance. This is to acknowledge that maybe we don't know best and that maybe the world is more than a playground for satisfying our desires. This is humility in action. "Humility means trusting the Tao, thus never needing to be defensive." And the more power you have, the more humble you need to be. At the level of the country, "the more powerful it grows, the greater the need for humility."

But what does humility in action look like? At the individual level, one way it shows is in how we handle mistakes. Does pride rule the day as we become obstinate and try to impose our will, acting with force if necessary? Or is there another way? This chapter gives us a four-step sequence for handling mistakes with humility. Realize it, admit it, correct it, and acknowledge that this is how you learn. This is typically hard for us to do.

Why? Because pride gets in the way. Pride is the self-image, or ego, which thinks it knows best and has desires it wants to satisfy. Would the ego handle mistakes as outlined above? Not a chance. Would it see the value in having others point them out? No way. It would see critics as enemies. It is only a "great man" who has mastered his ego who "considers those who point out his faults as his most benevolent teachers." The great man "thinks of his enemy as the shadow that he himself casts." He knows that the only real enemy lies within. In fact, the shadow is none other than the ego itself. The real question is, do we live in the shadow or in the light? Are we centered in the ego or centered in the Tao?

What does this look like as we progress from the level of the individual to the level of a country? "If a nation is centered in the Tao, if it nourishes its own people and doesn't meddle in the affairs of others, it will be a light to all nations in the world." Note the reference to "meddling"; it's like the reference to "poking" in the last chapter. "Governing a country is like frying a small fish. You spoil it with too much poking" (chapter 60).

In summary, power calls for humility, for dropping defenses, for admitting and learning from mistakes, and for not meddling and interfering with others. This is what humility looks like. Centered in the Tao, not in the ego—that's where the light is.

How often we do the opposite of trusting the Tao. We have our idea of the way things should be, and we hold onto it and defend it as we seek to impose our will. And how seldom we admit to mistakes, let alone learn from them.

Have you ever considered those who point out your faults to be your "most benevolent teachers"? It's hard to do this, isn't it? And the reason is that our defenses are up. This is why we see critics as enemies, not teachers. So what does it take to see them as teachers? In a word, humility. And it is not easy to be humble.

This chapter reminds us that "humility means trusting the Tao, thus never needing to be defensive." When we are centered in the Tao, our defenses can be down and we can welcome all things—even our most benevolent teachers.

62

The Tao is the center of the universe,
the good man's treasure,
the bad man's refuge.

Honors can be bought with fine words,
respect can be won with good deeds;
but the Tao is beyond all value,
and no one can achieve it.

Thus, when a new leader is chosen,
don't offer to help him
with your wealth or your expertise.
Offer instead
to teach him about the Tao.

Why did the ancient Masters esteem the Tao?
Because, being one with the Tao,
when you seek, you find;
and when you make a mistake, you are forgiven.
That is why everybody loves it.

The Tao is beyond all value.

How can the Tao be both "the good man's treasure" and "the bad man's refuge"? The answer is, the Tao is Oneness/Wholeness, which encompasses everything. At this level there are no distinctions between things, much less value judgments about whether some people are good and others bad. To make distinctions you have to stand apart and distance yourself from Oneness/Wholeness. Only then can you identify and separate things, make judgments about them, and start deciding to desire some and fear others. And that's where the trouble begins, because as soon as you stand apart, you're no longer centered in the Tao.

"The Tao is the center of the universe." We may recall, "If powerful men and women could remain centered in the Tao, all things would be in harmony" (chapter 32). To stand apart from it is to risk disturbing the balance. "Just stay at the center of the circle and let all things take their course" (chapter 19). So how do we stay centered? How can we be "one with the Tao"? This chapter gives some guidance.

For a start, the Tao is not to be confused with concepts like honor or respect, which you can achieve by doing certain things. For example, "Honors can be bought with fine words, respect can be won with good deeds." If you want them, you can buy them and win them. But we can't do this with the Tao, because "the Tao is beyond all value, and no one can achieve it." Thus it is neither buyable nor winnable nor achievable. This means neither our wealth nor our expertise can buy or win or achieve the Tao, either for ourselves or for anyone else, for that matter. So if you want to offer guidance to someone, "when a new leader is chosen, don't offer to help him with your wealth or expertise. Offer instead to teach him about the Tao."

Whenever we are not centered in the Tao, we're continually seeking harmony. We believe it's "out there" somewhere waiting for us to "achieve" it. We think it's something like honor and respect, which we have to buy and win. As long as we believe this, we'll continue to seek and never find. And we can spend our whole lives this way. Harmony comes from dwelling in the Tao. "Dwelling" isn't seeking with intent to find. It is simply "being one with."

When you are "one with the Tao," you are at the center. This means you're no longer standing apart. There is no separation. You are beyond seeking and finding. Or if you like, we could say "being one with the Tao, when you seek, you find." It doesn't matter how we say it. Similarly, you are beyond making what could be judged and labeled as mistakes. Or if you like, we could say, "Being one with the Tao[,] when you make a mistake, you are forgiven."

The Tao doesn't judge. We may recall, "The Tao gives birth to all beings, nourishes them, maintains them, cares for them, comforts them, protects them, takes them back to itself, creating without possessing, acting without expecting, guiding without interfering. That is why love of the Tao is in the very nature of things" (chapter 51). There's no mention here of mistakes, honor, respect, fine words, good deeds, wealth, or expertise. That's why the ancient Masters esteemed the Tao. "That is why everybody loves it." That's why it is in the "very nature of things."

Dwelling in the Tao is not about doing; it's about simply "being one with the Tao." At the center. No separation.

How often we value things like honor, respect, wealth, and expertise. At first glance, what's wrong with them? The answer is that, unless we're very careful, they can become serious distractions. Perhaps the most obvious is the pursuit of wealth. Less obvious is the pursuit of the esteem of others, for example, in the form of honor and respect. The problem is that these concepts have no meaning except in relation to what others think. And there's the trouble. They are not centered in the Tao.

Have you ever wondered how you would behave if you were the last person on earth? Honor and respect would have no meaning, would they? Of course, you might be distracted by the fact that there was no one else around, but, apart from that, what would guide your actions? What would you center yourself in?

This chapter reminds us that "the Tao is the center of the universe." When we are centered in it, we become one with it. There's nothing to buy or achieve. There is nothing to strive for. We're home. And this is true regardless of whether we're the last person on earth.

63

Act without doing;
work without effort.
Think of the small as large
and the few as many.
Confront the difficult
while it is still easy;
accomplish the great task
by a series of small acts.

The Master never reaches for the great;
thus she achieves greatness.
When she runs into a difficulty,
she stops and gives herself to it.
She doesn't cling to her own comfort;
thus problems are no problem for her.

Give yourself to your work.

The last chapter observed that "the Tao is the center of the universe" and harmony is to be found by "being one with the Tao." But what does this look like in practice? What do we do on a daily basis in our ordinary lives? The answer is, we do not "do" anything. However, this is not the same as doing nothing. What we do is "act without doing." And the difference is crucial.

It's easy to fill our ordinary lives with an endless stream of tasks. Typically, we have goals in mind, which we desire to achieve at some point in the future. We plan what we need to do and what we need others to do to help us achieve them. And then we get busy "doing things." The trouble is, we're never done. We may recall, "The ordinary man is always doing things, yet many more are left to be done" (chapter 38). Pursuing desires is an endless treadmill. Especially if they include a desire to inflate our egos by having others see us as "great."

In contrast, "The Master does nothing, yet he leaves nothing undone" (chapter 38). So how does he do this? What's more, how does he "work without effort"? The answer is "Because he has no goal in mind, everything he does succeeds" (chapter 22). It is stated similarly, "The Master . . . doesn't think about his actions; they flow from the core of his being" (chapter 50). The common denominator is no goal in mind, no thought, no preconceived plan, no particular expectation in the future. Instead, the Master engages in pure action in the here and now that flows in natural harmony with the Tao.

Interesting. But can you really achieve "great tasks" with this approach? Is it always smooth sailing? Not necessarily. However, handling difficulty need not be complicated. "Confront the difficult while it is still easy; accomplish the great task by a series of small acts." This is not so hard, really. It doesn't require a lot of thought.

And what happens if you encounter difficulty anyway? This is not a problem. It's only when we do things with particular expectations in mind that we tend to turn difficulties into problems. We do this by looking inside and clinging "to our own comfort." But we may recall, "He who clings to his work will create nothing that endures. If you want to accord with the Tao, just do your job, then let go" (chapter 24). So this is what the Master does. When she "runs into a difficulty, she stops and gives herself to it. She doesn't cling to her own comfort." She lets herself go. "Because she has let go of herself, she is perfectly fulfilled" (chapter 7).

And what is the outcome? "Thus problems are no problems for her." What's more, "the Master never reaches for the great; thus she achieves greatness." We may recall, "The Master doesn't try to be powerful; thus he is truly powerful. The ordinary man keeps reaching for power; thus he never has enough" (chapter 38). The difference lies in the reaching. Reaching is what happens the moment we have desires to achieve particular goals, make plans, have expectations, and start doing things.

Acting in harmony with the Tao requires none of this. "Giving birth and nourishing, having without possessing, acting with no expectations, leading and not trying to control; this is the supreme virtue" (chapter 10). We're back to the difference between acting and doing. We tend to get so hung up on doing. We need to not-do, as it were. We may recall, "Practice not-doing, and everything will fall into place" (chapter 3).

How often we get lost in an endless stream of daily tasks. We use phrases like "rat race," "treadmill," and "daily grind." The common denominator is that we're never done. We never arrive. Tomorrow is always more of the same. And our tasks are by no means "effortless." Some of them are difficult and take a lot of effort.

In fairness, not every task is like this. Have you ever lost yourself in some creative activity? Have you experienced hours go by that you weren't even aware of, when whatever you produced seemed to take very little effort on your part? Maybe you ran into difficulty, but you found a way to flow around it or perhaps even to creatively incorporate it.

This chapter reminds us that life is lived at the level of a series of small acts, each of which is an end in itself. They may add up to something others may choose to see as great. But that's not the point. Problems arise when we reach for greatness and think we can use the series of small acts as a means for getting there. All we need do is give ourselves to our work and we will be like the Master: "problems are no problems for her."

64

What is rooted is easy to nourish.
What is recent is easy to correct.
What is brittle is easy to break.
What is small is easy to scatter.

Prevent trouble before it arises.
Put things in order before they exist.
The giant pine tree
grows from a tiny sprout.
The journey of a thousand miles
starts from beneath your feet.

Rushing into action, you fail.
Trying to grasp things, you lose them.
Forcing a project to completion,
you ruin what was almost ripe.

Therefore the Master takes action
by letting things take their course.
He remains as calm
at the end as at the beginning.
He has nothing,
thus has nothing to lose.
What he desires is non-desire;
what he learns is to unlearn.
He simply reminds people
of who they have always been.
He cares about nothing but the Tao.
Thus he can care for all things.

Let things take their course.

When we dwell in the Tao we are rooted in the here and now. We are in touch with ourselves. We may recall, "If you let yourself be blown to and fro, you lose touch with your root. If you let restlessness move you, you lose touch with who you are" (chapter 26). Also, when we dwell in the present, we can respond immediately if we need to adjust our actions. "What is recent is easy to correct." Thus we are flexible instead of fixed and brittle, focused instead of scattered.

The way to prevent disharmony with the Tao is to nip it in the bud, "before it arises." How? By first creating order and pattern and then taking action. "Put things in order before they exist." This is how it is in nature. "The giant pine tree grows from a tiny sprout." But we do have to act. The journey of a thousand miles cannot start without our taking the first step. And when we take that first step, it's best to take it calmly.

Typically, much of our ordinary lives is filled with rushing to do things. We grasp for what we think we can possess. And if the things we do don't produce the results we want, then we apply more effort. As the saying goes, "If at first you don't succeed then try, try again." Unfortunately, often all we do is stubbornly try doing the same thing again and again. And it doesn't work. "Rushing into action, you fail. Trying to grasp things, you lose them." Projects and journeys have a natural pace to them, which cannot be rushed. "Forcing a project to completion, you ruin what was almost ripe."

So what does the Master do? Instead of rushing, he takes action calmly. He desires no prespecified outcome, thus he has nothing to rush for. "He remains as calm at the end as at the beginning." He has no particular expectation in mind, thus his action consists of "letting things take their course." We may recall, "The Master sees things as they are, without trying to control them. She lets them go their own way" (chapter 29). He does not grasp for possessions because he has none, desires none, and thus has nothing to lose. We may recall, "He lets all things come and go effortlessly, without desire" (chapter 55). "He doesn't think about his actions; they flow from the core of his being" (chapter 50).

How different this is from chasing after the desire of the moment. Our learned response is to rush into action trying to grasp things. It is as if we need to de-program ourselves. The Master knows this. "What he desires is non-desire; what he learns is to unlearn."

What matters is to stay rooted in the Tao, in touch with who you are. We may recall, "Whoever is planted in the Tao will not be rooted up" (chapter 54). And, "See the world as your self. Have faith in the way things are. Love the world as your self; then you can care for all things" (chapter 13). All we have to do is remember this idea and live it; preferably all the time. Although it's nothing new, it seems we need constant reminding. Hence the Master "simply reminds people of who they have always been."

All that matters is dwelling in the Tao and acting in harmony with it. Care about that instead of your particular desires, and you'll discover you can be open to everything. We may recall, "The Master doesn't seek fulfillment. Not seeking, not expecting, she is present, and can welcome all things" (chapter 15). The same idea is here: "He cares about nothing but the Tao. Thus he can care for all things."

How often we rush into action. It seems we have no patience for any delay between desire and fulfillment of that desire. And so we impose our will, force events in the world around us, and are surprised when things don't turn out exactly as we want, as quickly as we want.

Have you ever thought about how a pine tree grows? From tiny sprout to giant pine tree. How does that happen? Not by rushing. This chapter suggests that the tiny sprout represents the giant pine already "in order before it exists." And we create order before it exists every time we make a plan. This is how we "prevent trouble before it arises." And good plans take time.

This chapter reminds us that "the journey of a thousand miles starts from beneath your feet." But it starts calmly and proceeds and ends calmly. When we are centered in the Tao there is no rushing.

65

The ancient Masters
didn't try to educate people,
but kindly taught them to not-know.

When they think that they know the answers,
people are difficult to guide.
When they know that they don't know,
people can find their own way.

If you want to learn how to govern,
avoid being clever or rich.
The simplest pattern is the clearest.
Content with an ordinary life,
you can show all people the way
back to their own true nature.

The simplest pattern is the clearest.

Typically, we fill our minds with what we call knowledge. As we grow up, much of our education is spent learning what is already known. Some of us then choose to spend our lives researching what is as yet unknown and adding more to the structure of knowledge. We stand back and separate the things we observe, name them, and identify relationships between them. We ask questions and use our ever-increasing knowledge to find the answers. This can be both an interesting and a productive exercise.

But is a mind full of knowledge a prerequisite for living in harmony with the Tao? Well, the short answer is no, it's not. In fact, a mind full of anything tends to get in the way. "When they think they know the answers, people are difficult to guide." We may recall, "The Master leads by emptying people's minds and filling their cores" (chapter 3). We saw in the last chapter that, with respect to the Master, "What he desires is non-desire; what he learns is to unlearn" (chapter 64).

If education consists of filling people's minds with knowledge, then what the Master does is help people empty them. To do this he helps them "unlearn" or "not-know." Thus "the ancient Masters didn't try to educate people, but kindly taught them to not-know." What's more, the process is not so much one of educating as of guiding—and kindly guiding at that. Too often we are tempted to think that knowledge has all the answers and that more of it is the only way to go. But it's when people "know that they don't know" that their minds become quiet and they "can find their own way."

Thus guiding other people does not call for having more knowledge than they do, or more wealth for that matter. We may recall, "Thus, when a new leader is chosen, don't offer to help him with your wealth and expertise. Offer instead to teach him about the Tao" (chapter 62). With knowledge comes complexity that typically obscures the Tao. Instead, "the simplest pattern is the clearest." And clarity comes from within, from being centered in the Tao. "If powerful men and women could center themselves in it, the whole world would be transformed. People would be content with their simple, everyday lives, in harmony, and free of desire" (chapter 37).

The trouble with knowledge is that there's always more of it. With awareness of the Tao, there's less. We may recall, "In the pursuit of knowledge, every day something is added. In the practice of the Tao, every day something is dropped" (chapter 48). In fact there isn't really any "amount" of Tao at all. It simply is. However, it seems we find complexity more fascinating than simplicity. Chasing after knowledge in an effort to be clever, and chasing after material possessions in an effort to be rich can both be major distractions. Thus "if you want to learn how to govern, avoid being clever or rich," because these make for a complicated life. "Content with an ordinary life, you can show all people the way back to their own true nature." That's where the Tao is to be found. "That is why love of the Tao is in the very nature of things" (chapter 51).

How often we want answers. We never cease to question, and the pursuit of knowledge is our solution to almost any problem. And there's nothing wrong with it. However, as we've noted before, the trouble starts when we confuse what we know with everything there is and believe knowledge alone should guide all our actions. That's when we become "difficult to guide."

Have you ever thought about how much so-called knowledge we really need, to live in the world? Of course, knowledge helps to a point; but the point is far closer than we think. And what is on the other side is much greater than we think.

This chapter reminds us that "the simplest pattern is the clearest." It is when we are centered in the simplicity of the Tao rather than the complexity of our knowledge that we find our way back to our "own true nature."

66

All streams flow to the sea
because it is lower than they are.
Humility gives it its power.

If you want to govern the people,
you must place yourself below them.
If you want to lead the people,
you must learn how to follow them.

The Master is above the people,
and no one feels oppressed.
She goes ahead of the people,
and no one feels manipulated.
The whole world is grateful to her.
Because she competes with no one,
no one can compete with her.

Be humble.

The only power we have is the power to act. And our actions can upset, maintain, or restore harmony with the Tao. Often they do this by influencing others, and best is a subtle influence. Typically we think of power over others as a top-down hierarchy in which whoever is visibly on top has the highest command-and-control position. This chapter observes that true power lies in the humility of being lower, not higher, than others.

A natural analogy for this is water. We may recall, "The supreme good is like water, which nourishes all things without trying to. It is content with the low places that people disdain. Thus it is like the Tao" (chapter 8). Here we have the same image, with all streams flowing to the sea "because it is lower than they are. Humility gives it its power." Thus to govern people you need to place yourself humbly below them, not proudly above them. So, if anything, the model needs to be bottom-up rather than top-down.

Similarly, to lead people is not to be out in front of them imposing your own will. "If you want to lead the people, you must learn how to follow them." We may recall, "The Master has no mind of her own. She works with the mind of the people" (chapter 49). She doesn't expect people to follow her, and while she may "follow" or "work with" people at one level, at a deeper level the only thing she is following is the Tao.

But can government and leadership be "real" when they come from below and from following? We tend to imagine a leader as a bold individual with strong vision, out there in front of everyone issuing orders from on high through a chain of command. How else can it work? The short answer is, "If you want to be a great leader, you must learn to follow the Tao. Stop trying to control. Let go of fixed plans and concepts, and the world will govern itself" (chapter 57).

Really? Then what do you actually do as a leader? At the risk of sounding like a broken record, the answer is, you simply act in harmony with the Tao. In particular, none of your actions are designed to enhance your status as a leader in the eyes of others. We may recall, "When the Master governs, the people are hardly aware that he exists.

. . . The Master doesn't talk, he acts. When his work is done, the people say, 'Amazing: we did it, all by ourselves!'" (chapter 17).

In summary, government and leadership have nothing to do with the leader personally—only with his or her actions. As noted at the start of this chapter, the only power we have is the power to act. We may recall, "Thus the Master is content to serve as an example and not to impose her will" (chapter 58). Does it matter whether the Master is above or below the people? Not really; the result is that "no one feels oppressed." Does it matter if she is ahead or following? Not really; the result is that "no one feels manipulated."

Why does no one feel manipulated? Because the Master is not imposing her will. She has no personal agenda. It's not all about her. "The Master doesn't try to be powerful; thus he is truly powerful" (chapter 38). "When you are content to be simply yourself and don't compare or compete, everybody will respect you" (chapter 8). The idea here is the same. "Because she competes with no one, no one can compete with her." And the result? "The whole world is grateful to her."

Does the Master actually want people's respect and gratitude? No, of course not. Does he or she simply act in harmony with the Tao? Yes, absolutely. It's not complicated.

How often we concern ourselves with how to get others to do what we want. We believe that things are the way we see them, that our vision is the only one that matters, and that others simply need to be told what to do.

Have you ever had a boss or manager like that at work? That attitude isn't very inspiring, is it? Far better is a leader who articulates what becomes a common vision and then backs off and lets people work out the best way to implement it. Why is this more inspiring? Because the leader demonstrates trust. And trust calls for not thinking you always know best. In fact, leadership is about bringing out the best in others.

This chapter reminds us that leading to bring out the best in others calls for humility. When people share a common vision, there is no competition. No one feels oppressed. No one feels manipulated. What do people feel? Inspiration and gratitude.

67

Some say that my teaching is nonsense.
Others call it lofty but impractical.
But to those who have looked inside themselves,
this nonsense makes perfect sense.
And to those who put it into practice,
this loftiness has roots that go deep.

I have just three things to teach:
simplicity, patience, compassion.
These three are your greatest treasures.
Simple in actions and in thoughts,
you return to the source of being.
Patient with both friends and enemies,
you accord with the way things are.
Compassionate toward yourself,
you reconcile all beings in the world.

Simplicity, patience, compassion are all that matter.

The start of this chapter sounds defensive, doesn't it? Clearly the observations in these chapters have drawn criticism such as "nonsense" and "lofty but impractical." So this chapter starts with a reply. In a nutshell, you can call it what you like, but the proof of the pudding is in the eating; that is, try it for yourself and see. This serves as a good reminder that there's nothing abstract and theoretical about dwelling in the Tao.

At the end of the day, "dwelling" is a very practical matter. It's about what we do with our time and our actions. Do we spend our time reaching to grasp possessions and power, to satisfy our never-ending desires and keep our egos inflated? Or do we spend our time acting in harmony with the Tao? By the time we get to the end of the day, it has been either one or the other. That said, for many of us it's likely an unconscious and clumsy blend of both, depending on our level of awareness. Awareness aside, we're assured there's nothing superficial about the content of these chapters. However, the only way to know it is to live it, as opposed to talking about it: "to those who put it into practice, this loftiness has roots that go deep."

We already know the Master prefers to teach by example. "Teaching without words . . . that is the Master's way" (chapter 43), but this chapter makes an exception: "I have just three things to teach." What follows are "simplicity, patience, compassion." And then, for each in turn, a brief elaboration along with the consequence of applying it in daily life.

"Simple in actions and in thoughts, you return to the source of being." We already know simple is best. "In thinking, keep to the simple" (chapter 8). What's given here is the reason: because you return. "Return is the movement of the Tao. Yielding is the way of the Tao" (chapter 40). "Each separate being in the universe returns to the common source. Returning to the source is serenity" (chapter 16).

"Patient with both friends and enemies, you accord with the way things are." We may recall, "The Master . . . understands that . . . trying to dominate events goes against the current of the Tao" (chapter 30). Typically, our desires cause us to run out of patience because we are not content with the way things are and, like little children, we want to have our way and have it now.

"Compassionate toward yourself, you reconcile all beings in the world." Compassion is the opposite of desire. It's meeting the world where it is, not striving to reshape it into what we want it to be. We may recall, "The Master doesn't seek fulfillment. Not seeking, not expecting, she is present, and can welcome all things" (chapter 15). It's not about the parts and striving to possess them or control them, regardless of whether they are objects or other people. "The Master views the parts with compassion, because he understands the whole" (chapter 39). And with understanding and compassion comes the ability not only to welcome but also to reconcile.

As presented, each "treasure" is given along with the consequence of applying it in daily life. But we can also turn the sentences around and read them as a summary of the way to live in harmony with the Tao. In other words, the three things we need to do are "return to the source of being," "accord with the way things are," and "reconcile all beings in the world." Return, accord, reconcile. Then, if we ask how we do that, the answers are: be "simple in actions and in thoughts," be "patient with both friends and enemies," and be "compassionate toward yourself." Simplicity, patience, compassion. It works.

How often we complicate our world, have little patience, and act from desire to impose our will. As a result, we fail to center ourselves in the Tao, we do not "accord with the way things are," and we see "all beings in the world" as a means toward whatever end we have in mind at the time. Small wonder our hearts are not at peace and we find little serenity in our lives.

Have you ever studied something that just didn't seem to make sense until you tried it? The moment you did, you may have wondered what it was you didn't understand. But by then it really didn't matter, did it? Perhaps it's like reading about riding a bicycle and wondering how your body could possibly balance on two wheels. The moment you put the book down, try it, and succeed, you no longer even think about it. It doesn't need to make sense. You just do it.

This chapter reminds us that living in harmony with the Tao is a very practical matter. If you really want to, then you can try to make sense of it. But you don't have to. All you need do is put it into practice and experience the result. If you really want labels for what you're putting into practice, then you can have three: simplicity, patience, and compassion. But the labels are not the point. Living them is the point.

The best athlete
wants his opponent at his best.
The best general
enters the mind of his enemy.
The best businessman
serves the communal good.
The best leader
follows the will of the people.

All of them embody
the virtue of non-competition.
Not that they don't love to compete,
but they do it in the spirit of play.
In this they are like children
and in harmony with the Tao.

Live in the spirit of play.

This chapter is about being your best. And it asks, can you be your best without competing? We might also ask why it matters whether you compete or not. But let's look at the first question.

At first glance, "best" implies relativity. You can be the best athlete only relative to other athletes less good than you. The same holds for the best general, the best businessman, and the best leader. The question is, what does it take to be the best? And the answer is that it need not in fact be about the other athlete, the other general, the other businessman, or the other leader. Rather, it's about what you're doing when you're being the best, that is, your actions.

Following the will of the people is what the best leader does. Serving the communal good is what the best businessman does. Entering the mind of the enemy is what the best general does. So what does this mean? It means you're being your best without competing with others. "All of them embody the virtue of non-competition." All of them are not in fact about being better than anyone else. The actions are ends in themselves.

We may recall, "When you are content to be simply yourself and don't compare or compete, everybody will respect you" (chapter 8). Respect is a by-product. Desire for it is not the reason for your actions. In the same way, being the best athlete, the best general, the best businessman, or the best leader is a by-product of what you do. It's not the reason for doing it in the first place.

So this brings us back to the earlier question about why it matters whether you compete or not. And the answer is that it matters because of the spirit in which we act. Are you trying to beat the other guy so as to be seen as "the best," or are you simply being yourself and being the best you can be? The first is a competitive spirit; it's all about the other guy and how you are seen. The second is a playful spirit; it is all about you. It wouldn't actually matter if the other guy wasn't there. You'd still do what you'd do anyway. Hence the observation "Not that they don't love to compete, but they do it in the spirit of play."

Thus "the virtue of non-competition" is about not displaying yourself or proving yourself better than others or achieving a particular goal.

We may recall, "The Master, by residing in the Tao, sets an example for all beings. Because he doesn't display himself, people can see his light. Because he has nothing to prove, people can trust his words. . . . Because he has no goal in mind, everything he does succeeds" (chapter 22).

The difference between play and competition lies in the desire to win. The first is about exploring in harmony with the Tao while being content with the way you are. The second is about the desire to be seen in a certain light by others. We may recall, "Because he is content with himself, he doesn't need others' approval. Because he accepts himself, the whole world accepts him" (chapter 30). Contentment and acceptance is the critical difference.

"In harmony with the Tao . . . all creatures flourish together, content with the way things are" (chapter 39). This is what it's like when children play. Simple. Uncomplicated. No agendas, no ulterior motives, no self-consciousness, no desires. Just playing contentedly and dwelling in the moment. This is what it's like living in harmony with the Tao.

How often we compete with each other. Sometimes it's obvious, for example, anything to do with money or material possessions. Sometimes it's more subtle, for example, anything to do with status, such as job titles or names of people we know or the number of countries we've visited. But it's surprising in how many places we find competition.

Have you ever wondered how your life is going without comparing it to someone else's life? Sadly, we have a whole marketing industry with a vested interest in ensuring you keep comparing your life with some better version of it and falling short. But even when we ignore the marketers, we're left with an important question: What does it take for our life to be the best it can be? Just on its own, relative to nothing else. This is an interesting question.

This chapter reminds us that we're at our best when we are not centered in ourselves, anxious about being better than somebody else. We're at our best when we live in harmony with the Tao, content to be who we are, and when the spirit we live in is one of play rather than competition. Life doesn't get better than that.

69

The generals have a saying:
"Rather than make the first move
it is better to wait and see.
Rather than advance an inch
it is better to retreat a yard."

This is called
going forward without advancing,
pushing back without using weapons.

There is no greater misfortune
than underestimating your enemy.
Underestimating your enemy
means thinking that he is evil.
Thus you destroy your three treasures
and become an enemy yourself.

When two great forces oppose each other,
the victory will go
to the one that knows how to yield.

Know how to yield.

Is this chapter about how to win a military battle? Not really. It's about how success comes from yielding rather than imposing your will by force. So, is yielding the secret for success to winning the battle? Not really. Success is about maintaining or restoring harmony with the Tao.

We might ask, where is harmony when "two great forces oppose each other"? This is a good question. The answer is, it's nowhere in sight. No one is about to win, because ultimately there is no victory from violence. We may recall, "Peace is his highest value. If the peace has been shattered, how can [a decent man] be content?" (chapter 31). But if peace has been shattered and action needs to be taken, then the question becomes how best to restore harmony. Would it be better to use force or to yield?

The answer is yield. "Rather than make the first move it is better to wait and see. Rather than advance an inch it is better to retreat a yard." Really? What's the meaning of "going forward without advancing, pushing back without using weapons"? These words sound like a recipe for defeat. How does this approach promote victory?

There are two reasons this approach promotes victory. First, because force never works in the long run. We may recall, "Whoever relies on the Tao in governing men doesn't try to force issues or defeat enemies by force of arms. For every force there is a counterforce. Violence, even well intentioned, always rebounds upon oneself" (chapter 30). The second reason is that to use force is to presume to know the mind of your enemy. Most likely you don't, and by acting first and with force you lose the opportunity to find out. "There is no greater misfortune than underestimating your enemy." And how do we typically do this? By making assumptions such as "thinking that he is evil." This is a big mistake. Why?

Again, there are two reasons for this being a mistake. First, "His enemies are not demons, but human beings like himself. He doesn't wish them personal harm. Nor does he rejoice in victory. How could he rejoice in victory and delight in the slaughter of men?" (chapter 31). The second reason is that "you destroy your three treasures and become an enemy yourself" (This is a reference to "I have just three things to teach: simplicity, patience, compassion. These three are your greatest treasures," chapter 67.) Make the first move, advance an inch, use force to impose your will, and simplicity, patience, and compassion are destroyed in an instant.

So what do you do? "When two great forces oppose each other, the victory goes to the one who knows how to yield." We may recall, "Seeing into darkness is clarity. Knowing how to yield is strength" (chapter 52). "The soft overcomes the hard. The slow overcomes the fast" (chapter 36). "Return is the movement of the Tao. Yielding is the way of the Tao" (chapter 40).

But does yielding mean you don't do anything? Do you just stand there passively while "great forces" upset the Tao? Not at all. We may recall, "The Master allows things to happen. She shapes events as they come. She steps out of the way and lets the Tao speak for itself" (chapter 45). There's nothing passive about shaping. And it's very different from imposing your will by force.

Thus "the Master observes the world but trusts his inner vision" (chapter 12). His concern is not so much for estimating or underestimating his enemy as for restoring harmony. He yields, but he also acts. And, if necessary, "he enters a battle gravely, with sorrow and great compassion, as if he were attending a funeral" (chapter 31). Simplicity, patience, compassion, yielding. This is the way of the Tao.

How often we like to make the first move, to advance if only by an inch, and to push back if we don't succeed. We desire to impose our will on the world and, when the world does not oblige, we see ourselves in opposition to it. And so the struggle begins.

Have you ever noticed how we associate victory in a struggle with one force overpowering another? Similarly, we associate yielding with backing down, losing, giving in, or giving up. Why do we do this? I think we do so because we think in terms of winning and losing in the first place, and then we assume the fight goes to the strongest. What if we were wrong on both counts? What if there were no winning and losing, and what if there were no fight?

This chapter reminds us that, if we must think in terms of victory, then victory goes "to the one that knows how to yield." And there is only one thing to yield to, the Tao.

My teachings are easy to understand
and easy to put into practice.
Yet your intellect will never grasp them,
and if you try to practice them, you'll fail.

My teachings are older than the world.
How can you grasp their meaning?

If you want to know me,
look inside your heart.

Look inside your heart.

How do you dwell in the Tao? Well, you don't do it by trying to grasp the Tao intellectually. First, you'll never succeed. Second, there's no need. Dwelling in the Tao has nothing to do with a two-step process of intellectual grasping followed by diligent application of grasped teachings. With all due respect, the intellect does have its place. It's just not here.

"My teachings are easy to understand and easy to put into practice" as long as we sidestep the intellect. Indeed the Master does his best to help us avoid getting stuck here. We may recall, "The Master acts without doing anything and teaches without saying anything" (chapter 2). This is because as soon as words are in the air, the mind has something to grasp at. As soon as we grasp, we miss the point. Why? Because the point is not the words themselves, it's what they point to.

With respect to dwelling in the Tao, the mind with all its intellectual machinery gets in the way. "Thoughts weaken the mind. Desires wither the heart" (chapter 12). It would be better for us to get some distance. "Can you step back from your own mind and thus understand all things?" (chapter 10). This is a good question. And the answer is typically no. And so it's best to teach by example. "The Master, by residing in the Tao, sets an example for all beings" (chapter 22). This approach works better because there's nothing for the mind to grasp at. There are no words, fewer distractions.

In particular, the teachings are not about the Master himself. If he could, he'd be anonymous to avoid the potential distraction. The teachings are about recognizing the truth that's present in all of us. Thus the Master is not full of himself. He's empty of himself even to the point of not knowing who he is anymore. "Because he doesn't know who he is, people recognize themselves in him" (chapter 22). Who the Master is or what kind of life he leads really doesn't matter. "Content with an ordinary life, you can show all people the way back to their own true nature" (chapter 65). Showing people the way is what matters, for people to recognize what's already within them. "Love of the Tao is in the very nature of things" (chapter 51). Returning to that "very nature" is what the Master's example is all about.

Typically, we're so full of ourselves, what we think we know, and all the concepts we have grasped intellectually that the first thing we have to do is clear all that out of the way. Thus "the Master leads by emptying people's minds and filling their cores, by weakening their ambition and toughening their resolve. He helps people lose everything they know, everything they desire" (chapter 3). Only now are we empty and teachable. So now we're back to the opening line of this chapter, "My teachings are easy to understand and easy to put into practice."

And how exactly do we put the teachings into practice? Aha! The answer is, by recognizing that it's the mind that is asking the question. What's more, it wants an answer in words and concepts that it can grasp intellectually, perhaps a neatly prescribed process with steps to follow and levels to try to attain. But we're not fooled any more, are we?

Knowledge is not out there waiting to be grasped. It lies within. You already know all you need to know. You just need to recognize it. It's the same in you as it is in me, as it is in the Master. "If you want to know me, look inside your heart." Note, he does not say to look inside your intellect. At heart, we are all the same. "Empty your mind of all thoughts. Let your heart be at peace" (chapter 16). Intellect is not required.

How often we like to grasp things intellectually. Yet it seldom seems to occur to us that we can never grasp anything bigger than what we can wrap our minds around. If the Tao is the Oneness/Wholeness that is everything, how can we possibly even begin to grasp it? We don't stand a chance. But that doesn't keep us from trying.

Have you ever put something into practice without having grasped it intellectually first? Of course you have. How about your first steps as a child? There's nothing intellectual about standing up, lurching forward, wobbling, falling down, and repeating the sequence. In the end, you mastered it. Was your intellect required? I don't think so.

This chapter reminds us that putting the Master's teachings into practice is not an intellectual exercise. It is a purely practical one. The moment we realize this and sidestep the intellect, it becomes easy. We just do it.

71

Not-knowing is true knowledge.
Presuming to know is a disease.
First realize that you are sick;
then you can move toward health.

The Master is her own physician.
She has healed herself of all knowing.
Thus she is truly whole.

Not-knowing is true knowledge.

These are strong words. First we are told that our idea of knowledge is not "true knowledge." Then we are told it's no better than a "disease." These words sound like a slap in the face for the intellect. This chapter builds directly on the last one: "My teachings are easy to understand and easy to put into practice. Yet your intellect will never grasp them" (chapter 70). So if we had any lingering thoughts as to whether we might still approach the Tao through intellect and knowledge, there shouldn't be any doubt left now. It's definitely not the way to go!

Two questions spring to mind. First, why is our idea of knowledge merely "presuming to know" and not "true knowledge"? Second, why does it get labeled a "disease" and why do we get called "sick"? This chapter doesn't give much explanation, likely because this ground has been covered in earlier chapters. The short answer is that a mind full of what we call knowledge is full, and that's the problem, whereas "true knowledge" results from emptying the mind until there is nothing left but awareness of the Tao.

We may recall, "In the pursuit of knowledge, every day something is added" (chapter 48). This is how our minds get cluttered and the Tao gets obscured, and why true education does not consist of filling the mind with anything at all, let alone what we might call knowledge. "The ancient Masters didn't try to educate people, but kindly taught them to not-know. When they think they know the answers, people are difficult to guide" (chapter 65).

However, it's one thing to be called "difficult to guide" but quite another to be called "sick." Even if our idea of knowledge is no more than "presuming to know," why should it be labeled a "disease" that we need to be healed from? "The Master is her own physician. She has healed herself of all knowing." A clue lies in the words that follow: "Thus she is truly whole."

The trouble with so-called knowledge is that it cannot deal with Oneness/Wholeness. It can deal only with the separate pieces that it chooses to identify and name. Pieces can be grasped but the whole cannot. "My teachings are older than the world. How can you grasp their meaning?" (chapter 70). If this is true, then how has the Master been able to heal herself? The answer is, by emptying her mind and not presuming to know. "The Tao is ungraspable. How can her mind be at one with it? Because she doesn't cling to ideas" (chapter 21). Clinging to ideas, presuming to know, filling your head with so-called knowledge—they're all the same, and none of them leads to harmony with the Tao. "The more you know, the less you understand" (chapter 47).

So where does "true knowledge" lie? The answer is, within. "How do I know this is true? By looking inside myself" (chapter 54). This is why a sentence like "Not-knowing is true knowledge" makes no sense when looked at from the outside. "But to those who have looked inside themselves, this nonsense makes perfect sense" (chapter 67). The reason you can never find the Tao is that you're looking for it. "The Tao is nowhere to be found. Yet it nourishes and completes all things" (chapter 41). You cannot find Oneness/Wholeness and you can never know it. But you can be it. Thus "the Master keeps her mind always at one with the Tao; that is what gives her her radiance" (chapter 21).

The light is not to be found by looking outside. The fact that you persist in looking is the disease. "Use your own light and return to the source of light" (chapter 52). This is how to heal yourself and be truly whole.

How often we presume to know without realizing we're doing so. We don't think of our knowledge as presumption, because we believe it is real. We assume we're healthy and, if anything, we think of ignorance as a disease to be cured with education. This chapter suggests that it's the other way around. Really?

Have you ever thought about how children learn their first language? Their intellect is hardly developed, yet they learn. How do they do that? It's when they learn their second language, assuming they're older, that our approach to teaching them becomes intellectual. We "presume" they need to distinguish parts of speech and understand the rules of grammar, so this is what we teach them. But this isn't how they learned their first language, is it?

This chapter reminds us that "not-knowing is true knowledge." What's more, it suggests we won't get healthy until we realize knowledge can make us "sick." This is because knowledge breaks up reality into what we call understandable pieces, which we then presume to "know." But the finer the pieces, the further away they are from Oneness/Wholeness. This is why we have to "heal" ourselves of all knowing before we can be truly whole.

72

When they lose their sense of awe,
people turn to religion.
When they no longer trust themselves,
they begin to depend on authority.

Therefore the Master steps back
so that people won't be confused.
He teaches without teaching,
so that people will have nothing to learn.

Never lose your sense of awe.

The Tao is awesome. "The Tao gives birth to all beings, nourishes them, maintains them, cares for them, comforts them, protects them, takes them back to itself, creating without possessing, acting without expecting, guiding without interfering" (chapter 51). "It is always present within you. You can use it any way you want" (chapter 6). How can we lose a sense of awe? Yet, surprisingly, we do. And when that happens we have to replace it with something.

The standard replacement for a sense of speechless awe and wonder is organized religion, where there are lots of words for the mind to grasp, lots of concepts and ideas to cling to, and likely lots of rituals for those who want to do things. We may recall, "When the Tao is lost, there is goodness. When goodness is lost, there is morality. When morality is lost, there is ritual. Ritual is the husk of true faith" (chapter 38). Needless to say, harmony with the Tao does not lie in concepts, rituals, and husks. It lies in looking within, recognizing that what's there is the awesome Tao, and trusting it.

So why don't we look within and trust ourselves? Why do we look outside and place our faith in religion, cleverness, and knowledge instead? "When the great Tao is forgotten, goodness and piety appear. When the body's intelligence declines, cleverness and knowledge step forth" (chapter 18). Rather than trust ourselves, it seems we place our trust in others who are more "knowledgeable," and so we begin to turn them into authority figures. The people, "when they no longer trust themselves . . . begin to depend upon authority."

The Master now has a dilemma. He could step forward and remind people, "If you accept the world, the Tao will be luminous inside you and you will return to your primal self" (chapter 28). Your primal self runs on the "body's intelligence" in natural harmony with the Tao, free from the clutter of the knowledge-filled mind. But if he steps forward, then the Master risks being seen as an authority figure. He doesn't want to attract attention to himself. It's not about him. But people might not see it that way, and they might start to depend upon him. Hence his dilemma.

"Therefore the Master steps back so that people won't be confused." This is a good move. In fact, the further he steps back, the better. We may recall, "When the Master governs, the people are hardly aware that he exists" (chapter 17). That's the best. He doesn't even attract attention. He doesn't teach them anything new. He doesn't fill their minds with knowledge. "He simply reminds people of who they have always been" (chapter 64). No "teaching" actually takes place.

This is why "he teaches without teaching, so that people will have nothing to learn." Similarly, "The ancient Masters didn't try to educate people, but kindly taught them to not-know" (chapter 65). Education and teaching imply students filling their minds with knowledge learned from the Masters. Harmony with the Tao comes from emptying the mind, not filling it. Knowledge is the problem, not the solution. "Not-knowing is true knowledge" (chapter 71).

In the end, there's only one thing to learn. "If you open yourself to the Tao, you are one with the Tao and you can embody it completely. If you open yourself to insight, you are one with insight and you can use it completely" (chapter 23). That's all there is to it. It's not "knowledge" and it cannot be taught. It simply is. And it always was. There's no need to look for it. And the best way to recognize it is by example. "The Master, by residing in the Tao, sets an example for all beings. Because he doesn't display himself, people can see his light" (chapter 22). The light is already within you. Trust yourself. Never lose your sense of awe.

How often we lose our sense of awe. We've seen it all before. But we don't trust. We want to know what's going on and we want to be in charge. And so we invent knowledge, revere those who accumulate it, and turn them into authority figures. A good example is religion, which can be highly organized, with rules and rituals and judgments and high priests who tell us what to do. It seems we find this comforting.

When did you last lose yourself in awe and wonder at something— maybe a beautiful sunset, or a clear night sky, or simply being in among the big trees or in the mountains? Chances are, it was in natural surroundings. And chances are you fell silent. What's more, you didn't need anyone to tell you what to do.

This chapter reminds us that when the Master teaches, he will not be standing in the spotlight on center stage, impressing us with his knowledge of the constellations. He will simply point to the night sky and step out of the way.

73

The Tao is always at ease.
It overcomes without competing,
answers without speaking a word,
arrives without being summoned,
accomplishes without a plan.

Its net covers the whole universe.
And though its meshes are wide,
it doesn't let a thing slip through.

The Tao is always at ease.

Among other things, the Tao is a list of things we're typically not. For a start, we're usually restless, competitive, and talkative. If we arrive somewhere, it's usually in response to a desire to get there or to having been summoned. If we want to achieve a goal, we've usually visualized our desired outcome, made a plan full of things to do, and are in execution mode to accomplish the results. Restless, competitive, talkative, and focused on accomplishing. Let's look at each in turn and contrast them with the Tao.

For a start, "the Tao is always at ease," whereas we tend to be restless, always moving, never arriving, always wanting to be somewhere other than where we are. We may recall, "If you let yourself be blown to and fro, you lose touch with your root. If you let restlessness move you, you lose touch with who you are" (chapter 26). Dwelling in harmony with the Tao is all about being who we are, right here, right now, without going anywhere.

The Tao "overcomes without competing." Our typical approach is to strive to be "better than" whomever we think we're competing with. It's seldom about us simply being ourselves. If at first we don't win, then we try harder or faster. However, we may recall, "The gentlest thing in the world overcomes the hardest thing in the world" (chapter 43). "The soft overcomes the hard. The slow overcomes the fast" (chapter 36). This is the way of the Tao.

The Tao "arrives without being summoned." Unlike wherever we think we need to be, the Tao is already here, and it's going nowhere. No effort needs to be expended. We may recall, "The Master arrives without leaving, sees the light without looking, achieves without doing a thing" (chapter 47). He accepts the world as it is, with no goals or desires for it to be any different. No rushing about doing things. Just acting with compassion, in harmony with the Tao. "Because he has no goal in mind, everything he does succeeds" (chapter 22).

The Tao "accomplishes without a plan." Really? How can you succeed without a purposeful plan? The Master does it by accepting, acting with compassion, and letting go. That's all there is to it. There's not much for the restless mind to chew on. In fact, there's really not much to say about the Tao at all. "Words that point to the Tao seem monotonous and without flavor. When you look for it, there is nothing to see. When you listen for it, there is nothing to hear" (chapter 35). Thus the Tao "answers without speaking a word."

Unfortunately for the mind, the Tao cannot be separated into convenient pieces to be grasped and chewed on, because it is Oneness/Wholeness. "Its net covers the whole universe." Any pieces we identify are just artifacts of the mind's desire to make distinctions. And if we're not careful, this activity can be very distracting.

But can we trust the Tao? Of course we can. "The great Tao flows everywhere. All things are born from it, yet it doesn't create them. It pours itself into its work, yet it makes no claim. It nourishes infinite worlds, yet it doesn't hold onto them. . . . [It] is merged with all things" (chapter 33). And that includes us.

"And though its meshes are wide, it doesn't let a thing slip through." So we're safe. There's no need to compete or travel anywhere or make plans or strive to achieve goals. "Be content with what you have; rejoice in the way things are. When you realize there is nothing lacking, the whole world belongs to you" (chapter 44). There's no need to be restless. Just be like the Tao: at ease.

How often we are not at ease in our lives. We can be so busy competing and striving that we may even forget what being at ease feels like. We tell ourselves we will be happy and at ease when we have the next promotion or a bigger house, or when someone else does something with their lives that we think affects us.

Have you ever thought about how all these have one thing in common? They all depend on things in the future. None of them is here now. Hitch your happiness to them and you immediately push it out into the future too. And most likely it will stay there, if not for one reason, then for another. The result is that you will never be at ease right here and right now.

This chapter reminds us that the capability to be at ease is already here and now. And it depends on only one thing. Are we prepared to trust the Tao? We could ask, what's the alternative? After all, would we rather trust ourselves? Which does your track record suggest would be the better bet?

If you realize that all things change,
there is nothing you will try to hold on to.
If you aren't afraid of dying,
there is nothing you can't achieve.

Trying to control the future
is like trying to take the master carpenter's place.
When you handle the master carpenter's tools,
chances are that you'll cut your hand.

All things change.

Why is it we're typically uncomfortable with change? Who knows? It seems we'd rather have more of what we already know than risk change. We don't want surprises, whether we end up liking them or not. We'd rather have the predictability of knowing something in advance of its happening. And having things stay the same makes them totally predictable. In short, fear of change is all about knowing. It seems we like knowledge and don't like the lack of it.

But even if we want to prevent change, do we really think we can? The answer is yes. We think we can do it by holding on to things and by trying to control the future. This chapter tells us that not only will we fail, but we'll also get hurt in the process of trying. Why?

Nature is change. Seasons come and go. Rivers flow to the sea. "In harmony with the Tao . . . all creatures flourish together, content with the way they are, endlessly repeating themselves, endlessly renewed" (chapter 39). So we have two choices. We can live in harmony with the Tao and accept the change of endless renewal, or we can try to hold on to things and control them. Why would we do the latter? Do we really think we know better than the Tao? We often think we do.

An earlier chapter wondered, "Do you want to improve the world? I don't think it can be done. The world is sacred. It can't be improved. . . . The Master sees things as they are, without trying to control them. She lets them go their own way" (chapter 29). To hold on is to interfere. In the long term, it's futile. In the short term, by getting in the way of what we can do with each present moment it prevents us from dwelling in the Tao. This is because holding on to things from the past and dragging them into the present limits our ability to live in the here and now. "If you want to accord with the Tao, just do your job, then let go" (chapter 24). "True mastery can be gained by letting things go their own way. It can't be gained by interfering" (chapter 48).

Imagine we didn't fear change. A good example is death, the biggest change we'll all personally experience sooner or later. If we can overcome our fear of death, then surely we can overcome our fear of change. If we do this, we'll live fully in the present moment and will suddenly discover that the sky's the limit. "If you aren't afraid of dying, there is nothing you can't achieve."

The opposite of holding on in fear is letting go. "The Master does his job and then stops. He understands that the universe is forever out of control, and that trying to dominate events goes against the current of the Tao" (chapter 30). Why does the phrase "out of control" fill us with dread? All it means is that we're not in total control. Why not let go? What don't we trust?

Imagine the Tao as a huge, peaceful river on which we're being carried gently downstream in a canoe. Do we paddle carefully and gently, to subtly guide and shape our journey as we go with the flow? Or do we decide, for some bizarre reason, that the river is out of control and try to paddle frantically upstream so we can hold on to the same spot we were in yesterday, in spite of the fact that everything else has flowed on past us? The choice is ours.

This chapter gives us another image. "Trying to control the future is like trying to take the master carpenter's place. When you handle the master carpenter's tools, chances are that you'll cut your hand." So, to combine the images, your choices are to get blisters as you try to paddle upstream, or cut your hand on the carpenter's tools as you try to improve the world. Of course, your third choice could be to go with the flow. "Open yourself to the Tao, then trust your natural responses; and everything will fall into place" (chapter 23). So which choice will you make? It's up to you.

How often we try to control the future. We don't know what the future will bring, but we always have choices about what we do with that lack of knowledge. We can fear that the future will be somehow worse than the present. We can see it as an opportunity to impose our will in some form or other. But a third option is to meet the future with an open mind; that is, with no preconceptions at all. If we want to embrace reality as it is and discover our part in how it unfolds, an open mind is the only way to go.

Have you ever thought about death? Most of us fear it because it is the great unknown. When you die, the one thing you will no longer be able to hold onto is life. Without doubt you will have to let your life go sooner or later. But in the meantime, what if you were to let go of your fear of death instead? As the saying goes, "Do not fear death, rather the unlived life."

This chapter reminds us that if you try to hold on, you'll likely get hurt. And often we do, whereas if you let go and "aren't afraid of dying, there is nothing you can't achieve." The choice is ours.

When taxes are too high,
people go hungry.
When the government is too intrusive,
people lose their spirit.

Act for the people's benefit.
Trust them; leave them alone.

Trust people.

A whole chapter about taxation? Well, not entirely. The last chapter observed that all things change, and that to try and prevent them from doing so is not only futile but also likely painful. Our attempts to prevent change include holding on to things, trying to control the future, and interfering in various ways with the unfolding of the Tao. Each time we have the same intent, to keep things knowable and predictable.

Why are knowledge and predictability so important to us? The last chapter explored this in terms of our fear of change. This chapter does so in terms of our lack of trust. While subtly different in principle, in practice the desire for knowledge and predictability causes us to try to hold on and control the world around us.

Good examples of our attempts to control are all forms of government. These not only amount to interfering but also tend to backfire by having the opposite of the intended results, especially if we try to force things. We may recall, "Whoever relies on the Tao in governing men doesn't try to force issues or defeat enemies by force of arms. For every force there is a counterforce. Violence, even well intentioned, always rebounds upon oneself" (chapter 30).

Thinking we know better than the Tao, we tinker with the controls of government. However, "if you want to be a great leader, you must learn to follow the Tao. Stop trying to control. Let go of fixed plans and concepts, and the world will govern itself. The more prohibitions you have, the less virtuous people will be. The more weapons you have, the less secure people will be. The more subsidies you have, the less self-reliant people will be" (chapter 57). This chapter adds another example: "When taxes are too high, people go hungry." In short, trying to control things doesn't work.

Too much government intrusion in people's lives fails to have the desired result. "When the government is too intrusive, people lose their spirit." A government that thinks it knows better effectively distrusts people, and its actions tend to bring about exactly what it doesn't want. "If you don't trust the people, you make them untrustworthy" (chapter 17).

So what should we do? The answer is simple. Back off. Stop thinking we know better. Let go and stop interfering. "Act for the people's benefit. Trust them; leave them alone." In short, we should trust and be tolerant. "If a country is governed with tolerance, the people are comfortable and honest" (chapter 58).

Dwelling in harmony with the Tao means not imposing our ideas on the world, whether through government or any other means. We may recall, "The mark of a moderate man is freedom from his own ideas. . . . Nothing is impossible for him. Because he has let go, he can care for the people's welfare as a mother cares for her child" (chapter 59). This is a good image, because a mother's caring is entirely focused in the present moment. She makes no attempt to control the future, no attempt to hold on to anything. She has no hidden agenda, no personal goals. "The Master doesn't seek fulfillment. Not seeking, not expecting, she is present, and can welcome all things" (chapter 15).

To let go is to trust. "Have faith in the way things are. Love the world as your self; then you can care for all things" (chapter 13). Replace holding on with letting go. And replace controlling with caring. This is to dwell in the Tao.

How often we try to hold on and control. How often we intrude in each other's lives. Regardless of what is naturally unfolding, we tend to think we have a better idea. And so we intrude to impose our will.

Have you ever thought about how you intrude in your own life? Now there's a strange thought. But every time you replace the reality of what is, with an imagined future better version, and then act to try and close the gap you just created, that's exactly what you do. You intrude.

This chapter reminds us, "Act for the people's benefit. Trust them; leave them alone." We could add: act for your own benefit, trust the Tao, and let your life unfold on its own.

Men are born soft and supple;
dead, they are stiff and hard.
Plants are born tender and pliant;
dead, they are brittle and dry.

Thus whoever is stiff and inflexible
is a disciple of death.
Whoever is soft and yielding
is a disciple of life.

The hard and stiff will be broken.
The soft and supple will prevail.

Be soft and supple.

To dwell in harmony with the Tao is to be open, empty, silent, receptive, and ready to respond with compassion to whatever life may bring your way. Too often we are the opposite. In other words, we tend to be closed-minded, full of our own ideas of how things ought to be, vocal and noisy, controlling, and constantly seeking to satisfy our desires. Does this interfere with the unfolding of the Tao? You bet. How? We become rigid and fixed in a world that is forever changing and unfolding.

Interestingly, we don't start out that way. "Men are born soft and supple." We may recall, "He who is in harmony with the Tao is like a newborn child. Its bones are soft, its muscles are weak" (chapter 55). The trouble is, we lose our suppleness as we grow up. Our minds and intellects become "educated" as we fill ourselves with knowledge. We also fail to see that every step along this path is a step away from where we came from. We lose touch with our roots and who we are.

"Can you coax your mind from its wandering and keep to the original oneness? Can you let your body become supple as a newborn child's? Can you cleanse your inner vision until you see nothing but the light?" (chapter 10). This is our constant challenge. And to the extent that the answer is no, we become stiff and hard in an ever-changing world. This is not a good combination.

This chapter observes that to become stiff and hard is to become more dead than alive. "Men are born soft and supple; dead, they are stiff and hard." We might wonder if this is a penalty reserved specially for us. And the answer is no; it is the way of nature. "Plants are born tender and pliant; dead, they are brittle and dry." Then, just in case we still don't get it, the message is clearly spelled out: "Thus, whoever is stiff and inflexible is a disciple of death. Whoever is soft and yielding is a disciple of life." I think we get it now.

It's hard to read some other message between these lines, isn't it? There's not much ambiguity there. We might even say, not much "flexibility." But, joking aside, the message is simple. To become stiff and inflexible is to become dead in a world that is living. Really? Surely, with enough force and will-power, we can impose our ideas on the world and make it conform to our desires. Well you can certainly try, but don't hold your breath. "The hard and stiff will be broken. The soft and supple will prevail." This is not what we wanted to hear, is it?

So what are we to do? The opposite of imposing our will is allowing things to unfold. But note that this doesn't mean we have no part in the unfolding. We may recall, "The Master allows things to happen. She shapes events as they come. She steps out of the way and lets the Tao speak for itself" (chapter 45). Her approach is not one of pride in thinking she knows best, but one of humility, of being open, receptive, yielding. Thus, for the Master, "his constant practice is humility. He doesn't glitter like a jewel but lets himself be shaped by the Tao, as rugged and common as a stone" (chapter 39).

Do you want some other images? How about "fluid as melting ice. Shapable as a block of wood. Receptive as a valley. Clear as a glass of water" (chapter 15). Do you want to know how to be like that? "Close your mouth, block off your senses, blunt your sharpness, untie your knots, soften your glare, settle your dust. This is the primal identity" (chapter 56).

The newborn child still has its primal identity, soft and supple. And you can return to yours any time you choose.

How often we become stiff and hard in how we view the world. We become set in our ways. A good test is how we act in the face of change. Are we inflexible or are we soft, supple, and yielding?

Have you ever thought about yielding in terms other than of being overcome by something? Typically we don't. But what if we think of yielding in terms of being soft and supple? Being open to the way life is unfolding and looking for how we can act with compassion to guide and shape, rather than impose our will.

This chapter reminds us that this is how to embrace life. To do anything else, it suggests, is nothing short of embracing death.

As it acts in the world, the Tao
is like the bending of a bow.
The top is bent downward;
the bottom is bent up.
It adjusts excess and deficiency
so that there is a perfect balance.
It takes from what is too much
and gives to what isn't enough.

Those who try to control,
who use force to protect their power,
go against the direction of the Tao.
They take from those who don't have enough
and give to those who have far too much.

The Master can keep giving
because there is no end to her wealth.
She acts without expectation,
succeeds without taking credit,
and doesn't think that she is better
than anyone else.

The Tao is perfect balance.

Nature is in harmony. We tend to interfere and upset the balance. We don't do so every time, because we can act in harmony with the Tao if we choose to. It depends on where we're coming from. Are we acting with desire to control and impose our will, or acting in response to life and giving with no expectation of return? The first upsets the balance. The second is part of it.

This chapter uses the image of a bow to illustrate this idea. The top is bent down and the bottom curls up because a tight string connects them both. In-as-much as the top and the bottom bend by equal amounts, the bow "adjusts excess and deficiency so that there is perfect balance." Of course, this is just an image, because the bow doesn't actually "adjust" anything. That's just the way a bow is. It is what it is. And in this important respect it is like the Tao.

We may recall, "In harmony with the Tao, the sky is clear and spacious, the earth is solid and full, all creatures flourish together, content with the way things are, endlessly repeating themselves, endlessly renewed. When man interferes with Tao . . . the equilibrium crumbles" (chapter 39). Why? Because there's a difference between the symmetry of a bow and what people do. The first is a natural balance that simply is. The second is deliberate action done with intent. The difference lies in the intent and in how the action is done.

We've noted that a bow doesn't deliberately do anything; it has no intent. It just is. This is also true for the next sentence: "It takes from what is too much and gives to what isn't enough." No, it doesn't. Strictly speaking, we should insert the words "It is as if" at the start of the sentence. This is the difference between what the bow does and what people do.

When people act, it is not "as if" they take "from what is too much" and give "to what isn't enough"; there is no "as if." This is exactly what they intend to do. And this is where the balance gets upset. The action is done with intent to control and impose will against the natural harmony. "Those who try to control, who use force to protect their power, go against the direction of the Tao. They take from those who don't have enough and give to those who have far too much." People who do this get things back to front. What's more, their actions are typically premeditated and applied with force.

Acting in harmony with the Tao is the opposite. No thought is involved and no force is applied. We may recall, "The Master gives himself up to whatever the moment brings. . . He doesn't think about his actions; they flow from the core of his being. He holds nothing back from life" (chapter 50). We may wonder how he can afford to hold nothing back. And the answer is, because he is acting in harmony with the Tao and "the Tao is . . . inexhaustible. . . . It is always present within you. You can use it any way you want" (chapter 6). The same idea is here. "The Master can keep giving because there is no end to her wealth."

She too holds nothing back, because she has let go. She seeks no credit, no return on her investment. "The Master doesn't seek fulfillment. Not seeking, not expecting, she is present, and can welcome all things" (chapter 15). She's not trying to prove anything, possess anything, or compete against anyone or anything. "Because she competes with no one, no one can compete with her" (chapter 66). Thus "she acts without expectation, succeeds without taking credit, and doesn't think that she is better than anyone else." This is what perfect balance looks like.

How often we upset the balance. Sometimes we do it on purpose, sometimes unwittingly. But it's usually because, in some way or another, we don't see life as an opportunity for giving. We see it as an opportunity for taking whatever it is that will satisfy the desire of the moment.

Have you ever held back from giving for fear you will run out? If we use money as an example, you might fear running out of money. But, on a level other than money, what is it that we fear we will run out of? The one thing we will definitely run out of, as time progresses, is the opportunity to give.

This chapter reminds us that when we give, something surprising happens. We do not run out. Instead, we somehow receive yet more to give. "The Master can keep giving because there is no end to her wealth." What if life were all about giving with no expectation in mind, no seeking of credit, no desire to be seen as "better than anyone else?" Just giving, letting go, and discovering you have yet more to give. That would be a perfect balance, wouldn't it?

78

Nothing in the world
is as soft and yielding as water.
Yet for dissolving the hard and inflexible,
nothing can surpass it.

The soft overcomes the hard;
the gentle overcomes the rigid.
Everyone knows this is true,
but few can put it into practice.

Therefore the Master remains
serene in the midst of sorrow.
Evil cannot enter his heart.
Because he has given up helping,
he is people's greatest help.

True words seem paradoxical.

Remain serene.

A couple of chapters ago we were reminded how yielding is the way of the Tao. It's also the opposite of being hard and inflexible. The first is the way of life, the second of death. "Men are born soft and supple; dead, they are stiff and hard. . . . Thus whoever is stiff and inflexible is a disciple of death. Whoever is soft and yielding is a disciple of life" (chapter 76).

What's more, "the hard and stiff will be broken. The soft and supple will prevail" (chapter 76). And it's the soft and supple that will break the hard and stiff. This chapter uses the image of water to make this point. "Nothing in the world is as soft and yielding as water. Yet for dissolving the hard and inflexible, nothing can surpass it. The soft overcomes the hard; the gentle overcomes the rigid." Life will prevail over death.

But what's meant by the next sentence? "Everyone knows this is true, but few can put it into practice." Putting it into practice means living our lives in such a way that we too are soft, supple, and yielding, like water. So how do we do that? The answer is, we let go of acting in response to desire. We give up expecting particular outcomes from our actions, competing to prove ourselves better than others, clinging to a need for particular results from what we do. Thus the Master "acts without expectation, succeeds without taking credit, and doesn't think she is better than anyone else" (chapter 77). She simply acts with compassion, in harmony with the Tao, and lets go. That's what putting it into practice means.

And what's the result? In short, harmony with the Tao. The point is that the Master succeeds because he has let go of desire, expectation, competition, and the need for particular results. "Nothing is impossible for him. Because he has let go, he can care for people's welfare as a mother cares for her child" (chapter 59). As it says here, "Because he has given up helping, he is people's greatest help." It's precisely because he has let go and given up that he succeeds.

This sounds paradoxical, doesn't it? As this chapter says, "True words seem paradoxical." No kidding. But they're true nonetheless. Similarly, "when the ancient Masters said, 'If you want to be given everything, give everything up,' they weren't using empty phrases" (chapter 22). The idea here is the same. We may recall, "Some say that my teaching is nonsense. Others call it lofty but impractical. But to those who have looked inside themselves, this nonsense makes perfect sense. And to those who put it into practice, this loftiness has roots that go deep" (chapter 67). Dwelling in harmony with the Tao is rooted in the practical. It really doesn't matter whether it makes sense or not.

Having let go of desire, the Master is always at one with the Tao, regardless of what's around him. "Therefore the Master remains serene in the midst of sorrow." He would be just as serene in the midst of happiness. We may recall, "She who is centered in the Tao can go where she wishes, without danger. She perceives the universal harmony, even amid great pain, because she has found peace in her heart" (chapter 35).

And once there is peace in the heart, there is no room for anything else. As this chapter says of the Master, "Evil cannot enter his heart." Why? Because his heart is full of whatever he cares about. "He cares about nothing but the Tao. Thus he can care for all things" (chapter 64).

How often it seems we care about anything but the Tao. We care more about what we desire and how to impose our will to bring it about. We may use noble words like "single-minded" and "determined," but they're not far removed from "hard" and "inflexible," are they?

Have you ever thought about how water not only flows around hard obstacles but eventually dissolves them? Its time frame for doing this, of course, is far greater than our typical attention span. It takes a long, long time. But the point is, in the short term, obstacles do not stop water dead in its tracks. They do not cause the water to rise up in opposition, as it were. The water doesn't "do" anything; it just flows around.

This chapter reminds us that we can put this idea into practice in our lives. And when we do, what we experience is serenity. It doesn't matter what obstacles are around us—evil, sorrow, even the desire to help others. It is when we give up desire and live in harmony with the Tao that we become serene and so, paradoxically, are the greatest help to others.

79

Failure is an opportunity.
If you blame someone else,
there is no end to the blame.

Therefore the Master
fulfils her own obligations
and corrects her own mistakes.
She does what she needs to do
and demands nothing of others.

Correct your own mistakes.

We all make mistakes. Even the Master, apparently. The question is, what do we do about them? There are at least two alternatives. The first is to take responsibility, look inside, and then do what you need to do to fix them. The second is to disown the responsibility by looking outside for someone else to pin it on, and thereby avoid the obligation to do the fixing. The second alternative is called blaming.

Blaming is a potentially endless game, because whomever you blame can likely blame someone else, and so on. "If you blame someone else, there is no end to the blame." If we're not careful, we can create a whole chain of blame while, in the meantime, of course, the original mistake remains unfixed.

The trouble starts with how the mistake is perceived. Is it a problem or an opportunity? If it's seen as a problem, then the inclination is to want to make it someone else's problem by blaming the mistake on them, which is essentially a negative response. On the other hand, if the mistake is seen as an opportunity, then we're more inclined to take ownership and fix it, which is essentially a positive response. This chapter invites us to see mistakes positively. "Failure is an opportunity." But, regardless of how we see it, we shouldn't lose sight of the fact that it's still "our" failure. Blaming is a deliberate attempt to lose sight of this fact. The truth is, it's still our responsibility.

What is a "failure"? What is a "mistake"? We may recall, "Prevent trouble before it arises. Put things in order before they exist.... Rushing into action, you fail. Trying to grasp things, you lose them. Forcing a project to completion, you ruin what was almost ripe" (chapter 64). These are examples of failures or mistakes, and what they have in common is that they go against the current of the Tao. So suppose we've failed to prevent trouble before it arises or, for whatever reason, we've failed to put things in order before they exist. We now have a failure on our hands. How can this be perceived positively?

The answer is that this "failure" represents an opportunity to act more effectively than we did first time around. We have the opportunity not only to see that we're the ones who need to do the acting (as opposed to anyone else), but also to see that there's no need to waste a moment looking over our shoulders before we get on with it. We may recall, "What is rooted is easy to nourish. What is recent is easy to correct" (chapter 64). Acting quickly ensures that the mistake remains recent. "Therefore the Master fulfils her own obligations and corrects her own mistakes."

Why don't we always do this? Because it depends on what we're rooted in and what we care about. If we care about the approval of others, then we're constantly trying to impress them. If we make mistakes, then we want to disassociate ourselves from what we've done, because we don't want to be seen in a bad light. This is the motivation for blaming. It's also the result of believing more in what we think others think of us than in what we believe about ourselves. In contrast, "because he believes in himself, [the Master] doesn't try to convince others. Because he is content with himself, he doesn't need others' approval. Because he accepts himself, the whole world accepts him" (chapter 30).

This is why the Master doesn't look over her shoulder before she acts. She has no need to. She's rooted in herself. So she simply gets on with it. "She does what she needs to do and demands nothing of others." Dwelling in harmony with the Tao means you're still responsible for your actions.

How often we prefer to blame others for our failures. That's much easier than taking responsibility for them, isn't it? Now we can take the easy path of complaining rather than the more difficult path of doing something about them.

Have you ever made a mistake when there was no around to blame? Likely there was also no one around to notice, so you wouldn't have needed to worry about losing face. But what did you do? Most likely you simply got on with whatever you needed to do to fix the situation. And you likely didn't waste much time over it either. After all, what else was there to do?

This chapter reminds us that we will make mistakes and that correcting them has nothing to do with anyone else. It is always up to us.

80

If a country is governed wisely,
its inhabitants will be content.
They enjoy the labor of their hands
and don't waste time inventing
labor-saving machines.
Since they dearly love their homes,
they aren't interested in travel.
There may be a few wagons and boats,
but these don't go anywhere.
There may be an arsenal of weapons,
but nobody ever uses them.
People enjoy their food,
take pleasure in being with their families,
spend weekends working in their gardens,
delight in the doings of the neighborhood.
And even though the next country is so close
that people can hear its roosters crowing and its dogs barking,
they are content to die of old age
without ever having gone to see it.

Be content with the way things are.

What does wise government look like? One way to tell is to look at the results. Are the people content? If so, we can say the country is fortunate to have a "wise" government that practices moderation and tolerance. We may recall, "For governing a country well there is nothing better than moderation" (chapter 59). "If a country is governed with tolerance, the people are comfortable and honest" (chapter 58).

If this is what wise government looks like, what do the country's contented inhabitants look like? The short answer is, they look like people living in natural harmony with the Tao, accepting the world as it is, and not trying to force their desires on it. It's said of the Tao that "if powerful men and women could center themselves in it, the whole world would be transformed by itself, in its natural rhythms. People would be content with their simple, everyday lives, in harmony, and free of desire. When there is no desire, all things are at peace" (chapter 37).

What follows is a longer answer describing what "simple everyday lives" look like. For example, centered in the Tao, people "act without doing; work without effort" (chapter 63), thus labor is not tiresome drudgery to be minimized. Instead, people "enjoy the labor of their hands and don't waste time inventing labor-saving machines."

Contented people are in touch with who they are and have no need to travel from restlessness. We may recall, "Thus the Master travels all day without leaving home. However splendid the views, she stays serenely in herself. . . . If you let yourself be blown to and fro, you lose touch with your root. If you let restlessness move you, you lose touch with who you are" (chapter 26). Contented people haven't lost touch with their roots. They're not about to be blown anywhere.

"People enjoy their food, take pleasure in being with their families, spend weekends working in their gardens." This and the following lines are the rest of the longer answer to what contented people look like. What they all have in common is freedom from restlessness and desire, acceptance of the world as it is, and a simple delight in living fully in the present moment. Thus "be content with what you have; rejoice in the way things are. When you realize there is nothing lacking, the whole world belongs to you" (chapter 44).

When there's nothing lacking, there's no desire. There's also no need to travel anywhere else. And anywhere else need not even be some exotic, distant land; it can be the country right next door that "is so close that people can hear its roosters crowing and its dogs barking." It doesn't matter. You still have no need to go there. You are "content to die of old age without ever having gone to see it."

So the question is, what's our part in making this happen? And perhaps there's no better summary than the following: "In dwelling, live close to the ground. In thinking, keep to the simple. In conflict, be fair and generous. In governing, don't try to control. In work, do what you enjoy. In family life, be completely present. When you are content to be simply yourself and don't compare or compete, everybody will respect you" (chapter 8).

If we act in this way, our simple, everyday lives will bring us peace and contentment. And if our government encourages us and doesn't get in our way, then we can call it "wise."

How often we look elsewhere for peace and contentment. If we're not experiencing it, then it must be somewhere else. So we need to go looking to find it. But what if it were under our feet all along? Then we'd completely miss it, wouldn't we? And that's what we do a lot of the time.

Have you ever gone looking for something, only to find it was in the most obvious place, right in front of you all the time? For instance, looking for your glasses only to find they were propped up on your own forehead all along. If peace and contentment were right in front of us all the time, what would they look like?

This chapter reminds us that they'd look exactly like our simple, everyday lives when we're living in harmony with the Tao. They're not somewhere else. They're right here.

81

True words aren't eloquent;
eloquent words aren't true.
Wise men don't need to prove their point;
men who need to prove their point aren't wise.

The Master has no possessions.
The more he does for others,
the happier he is.
The more he gives to others,
the wealthier he is.

The Tao nourishes by not forcing.
By not dominating, the Master leads.

Give to others.

Words are not the best for communicating about anything bigger than can be put into words. Whenever we try to use them to do so, words either seem paradoxical or stop making sense or, at the very least, aren't "eloquent." For example, "Because [the Master] has given up helping, he is people's greatest help. True words seem paradoxical" (chapter 78). Earlier, "Some say that my teaching is nonsense. . ." (chapter 67). And this chapter starts, "True words aren't eloquent; eloquent words aren't true."

Words work well only when we're talking about knowledge. This is because knowledge is all about separating, analyzing, identifying, distinguishing, and naming things. And we can do none of this without words. But does knowledge help us dwell in harmony with the Tao? No, not really. Thus if "true knowledge" is simply harmony with the Tao, then all this so-called knowledge can be a serious distraction. Or, to put it more strongly, we may recall, "Not-knowing is true knowledge. Presuming to know is a disease" (chapter 71).

This is why those who "truly know" realize that what they know cannot be put into words. Thus "those who know don't talk. Those who talk don't know" (chapter 56). Or, as this chapter observes, "Wise men don't need to prove their point; men who need to prove their point aren't wise." Dwelling in harmony with the Tao is not about proving anything. It's about dwelling in harmony with the Tao. End of story.

We may recall, "The Master, by residing in the Tao, sets an example for all beings. Because he doesn't display himself, people can see his light. Because he has nothing to prove, people can trust his words" (chapter 22). "Therefore the Master acts without doing anything and teaches without saying anything" (chapter 2). With all due respect to words, they're simply not needed. In fact, the less said, the better.

If dwelling in the Tao has nothing to do with words and knowledge, it also has nothing to do with desire. Once we "truly know" this, then we become free of both knowledge and desire and we can let go. When we do, suddenly everything simplifies as we stop trying to grasp and hold on to possessions or trying to force the world to be anything other than what it is. Thus "the Master has no possessions. The more he does for others, the happier he is. The more he gives to others, the wealthier he is" (There's another example of words being "paradoxical.")

So if the Master acts in harmony with the Tao, then how does the Tao act? The answer is, "The Tao nourishes by not forcing." We may recall, "The great Tao flows everywhere. All things are born from it, yet it doesn't create them. It pours itself into its work, yet it makes no claim. It nourishes infinite worlds, yet it doesn't hold on to them" (chapter 34). The Master does the same thing. He doesn't force. "By not dominating, the Master leads." Thus "the Master allows things to happen. She shapes events as they come. She steps out of the way and lets the Tao speak for itself" (chapter 45).

Are all eloquent words "not true"? Well, in spite of their limitations, perhaps some words that do a good job nonetheless are the following: "I have just three things to teach: simplicity, patience, compassion" (chapter 67). If any words have to be said, then these just about say it all.

So we have reached the end of the last chapter of the *Tao Te Ching*. And we have used many words along the way. Is there anything left to be said? The short answer is no. Simplicity, patience, compassion. That's what it takes to live in harmony with the Tao.

We may recall, "The Master . . . steps out of the way and lets the Tao speak for itself" (chapter 45). So now it's time for us to do exactly that. Enough said. Let the Tao speak for itself.

About the Author

FRANCIS PRING-MILL presents ideas in understandable ways to help others gain insights. He has been fascinated by the *Tao Te Ching* since discovering a copy in a secondhand store as a teenager. In this book he applies skills developed as a professional facilitator, course developer and instructor, and communicator to offer the reader a guided journey into a densely written ancient spiritual text.

In Harmony with the Tao is the product of analytical thinking combined with a creative talent for explaining ideas. The result will appeal to anyone interested in understanding the ideas contained in the *Tao Te Ching* and in applying them to daily life in the modern world.

Francis Pring-Mill has a master's degree and a doctorate from the University of Oxford, where he also won a postgraduate scholarship which funded three years of doctoral research. He then held a two-year postdoctoral fellowship at the University of Toronto. In the business world, his roles have included government statistician, software engineer, and director in an IT professional services firm. He has published in the fields of zoology, software engineering, and methodology. His writing is characterized by success at analyzing, simplifying, and presenting ideas to make them easier to understand and apply. In this book, he brings the same skills to a new subject.

If you have enjoyed this book, please consider leaving an online review.

To receive the author's newsletter, please sign up at
www.inharmonywiththetao.com

Printed in the USA
CPSIA information can be obtained
at www.ICGtesting.com
LVHW042253120324
774327LV00006B/137